EASY GUITAR WITH TAB

MAR 2 7 2015

THE GRAMMY AWARDS®

RECORD OF THE YEAR
1958 – 2011

D1217745

Visit The Recording Academy Online at
www.grammy.com

ISBN 978-1-4803-5423-4

HAL•LEONARD® CORPORATION

7777 W. BLUEMOUND RD. P.O. BOX 13819 MILWAUKEE, WI 53213

Visit Hal Leonard Online at
www.halleonard.com

>> Adele at the 54th GRAMMY Awards

THE RECORDING ACADEMY®

When it comes to music on TV, the last few years alone have seen some very memorable moments: Paul McCartney, Bruce Springsteen, Dave Grohl, and Joe Walsh jamming on "The End" from the Beatles' classic *Abbey Road*; Adele making her triumphant first live singing appearance after throat surgery to perform "Rolling In The Deep"; Pink dripping wet and hovering 20 feet above the stage while singing a note-perfect version of "Glitter In The Air"; and Lady Gaga hatching from a massive egg to perform "Born This Way." All of these performances, and many more, took place on the famed GRAMMY Awards® stage.

The GRAMMY® Award is indisputedly the most coveted recognition of excellence in recorded music worldwide. Over more than half a century, the GRAMMY Awards have become both music's biggest honor and Music's Biggest Night®, with the annual telecast drawing tens of millions of viewers nationwide and millions more internationally.

And with evolving categories that always reflect important current artistic waves — such as dance/electronica music — as well as setting a record for social TV engagement in 2012, the GRAMMYs keep moving forward, serving as a real-time barometer of music's cultural impact.

The Recording Academy is the organization that produces the GRAMMY Awards. Consisting of the artists, musicians, songwriters, producers, engineers, and other professionals who make the music you enjoy every day on the radio, your streaming or download services, or in the concert hall, The Academy is a dynamic institution with an active agenda aimed at supporting and nurturing music and the people who make it.

Whether it's joining with recording artists to ensure their creative rights are protected, providing ongoing professional development services to the recording community or supporting the health and well-being of music creators and music education in our schools, The Recording Academy has become the recording industry's primary organization for professional and educational outreach, human services, arts advocacy, and cultural enrichment.

The Academy represents members from all corners of the professional music world — from the biggest recording stars to unsung music educators — all brought together under the banner of building a better creative environment for music and its makers.

>> Paul McCartney at the 2012 MusiCares Person of the Year gala in his honor

>> Trombone Shorty and Mavis Staples at the GRAMMY Foundation's Music Preservation Project event in 2012

MUSICARES FOUNDATION®

MusiCares® was established by The Recording Academy to provide a safety net of critical assistance for music people in times of need. MusiCares has developed into a premier support system for music people, providing resources to cover a wide range of financial, medical and personal emergencies through innovative programs and services, including regular eBay auctions of one-of-a-kind memorabilia that are open to the public. The charity has been supported by the contributions and participation of artists such as Neil Diamond, Aretha Franklin, Paul McCartney, Bruce Springsteen, Barbra Streisand, and Neil Young — just to name the organization's most recent annual Person of the Year fundraiser honorees — and so many others through the years.

THE GRAMMY FOUNDATION®

The GRAMMY Foundation's mission is to cultivate the understanding, appreciation and advancement of the contribution of recorded music to American culture. The Foundation accomplishes this mission through programs and activities designed to engage the music industry and cultural community as well as the general public. The Foundation works to bring national attention to important issues such as the value and impact of music and arts education and the urgency of preserving our rich cultural legacy, and it accomplishes this work by engaging music professionals — from big-name stars to working professionals and educators — to work directly with students.

» Secretary of the Department of Health and Human Services Kathleen Sebelius and Recording Academy President/CEO Neil Portnow present the Recording Artists' Coalition Award to John Mayer at the GRAMMYs on the Hill Awards in Washington, D.C. in 2012

Paul Morigi/WireImage.c

FIGHTING FOR MUSICIANS' RIGHTS

Over the last 15 years, The Recording Academy has built a presence in the nation's capital, working to amplify the voice of music creators in national policy matters. Today, called the "supersized musicians lobby" by *Congressional Quarterly*, The Academy's Advocacy & Industry Relations office in Washington, D.C., is the leading representative of the collective world of recording professionals — artists, songwriters, producers, and engineers — through its GRAMMYs on the Hill® Initiative. The Academy has taken a leadership role in the fight to expand radio performance royalties to all music creators, worked on behalf of musicians on censorship concerns and regularly supported musicians on legislative issues that impact the vitality of music.

THE GRAMMY MUSEUM®

Since opening its doors in December 2008, the GRAMMY Museum has served as a dynamic educational and interactive institution dedicated to the power of music. The four-story, 30,000-square foot facility is part of L.A. Live, the premier sports and entertainment destination in downtown Los Angeles. The Museum serves the community with interactive, permanent and traveling exhibits and an array of public and education programs. We invite you to visit us when you're in the Los Angeles area.

As you can see, The Recording Academy is so much more than the annual GRAMMY telecast once a year, even if that one show is Music's Biggest Night. To keep up with all The Academy's activities, visit GRAMMY.com regularly, and join the conversation on our social networks:

 Facebook.com/TheGRAMMYs

 Twitter.com/TheGRAMMYs

 YouTube.com/TheGRAMMYs

 TheGRAMMYs.tumblr.com

 Foursquare.com/TheGRAMMYs

 Instagram (user name: TheGRAMMYs)

 Google+ (gplus.to/TheGRAMMYs)

TABLE OF CONTENTS (ALPHABETICAL)

TABLE OF CONTENTS (CHRONOLOGICAL)

All I Wanna Do

Words and Music by Kevin Gilbert, David Baerwald, Sheryl Crow, Wyn Cooper and Bill Bottrell

Strum Pattern: 5
Pick Pattern: 4

Spoken: Hit it.
Lyrics in italic are spoken throughout.

This ain't no disco.

It ain't no country club either.

This is L. A.

1. "All I wanna do is have a little fun before I die," says the man next to me out of nowhere, apropos of nothing he says his name is William, but I'm sure he's Bill or Billy or Mac or Buddy. But he's

E7

plain ugly to me, and I wonder if he's ever had a day of fun in his whole life.
2. *I like a good beer buzz early in the mornin' and Billy likes to peel the labels from his*

C7

D7   E7

bottles of Bud.
                 We are drinking beer at noon on Tuesday in a
                 He shreds them on the bar, then he lights ev'ry match in an over - sized

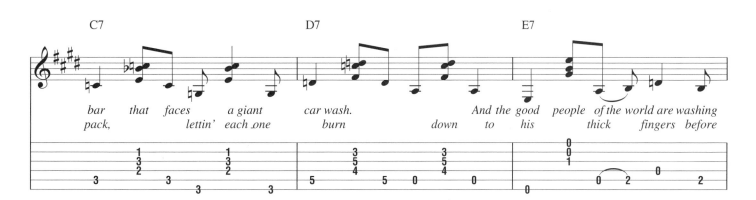

C7   D7   E7

bar that faces a giant car wash. And the good people of the world are washing
pack, lettin' each one burn down to his thick fingers before

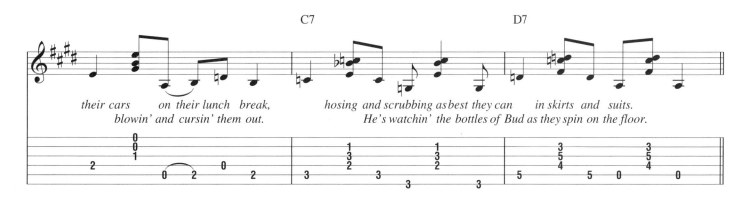

                     C7   D7

their cars on their lunch break, hosing and scrubbing as best they can in skirts and suits.
blowin' and cursin' them out. He's watchin' the bottles of Bud as they spin on the floor.

Pre-Chorus

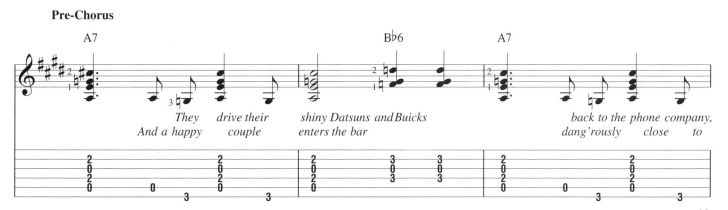

A7   B♭6   A7

They drive their shiny Datsuns and Buicks back to the phone company,
And a happy couple enters the bar dang'rously close to

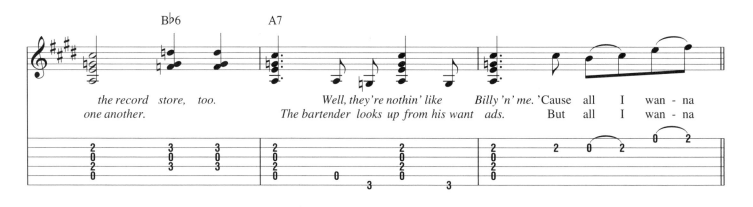

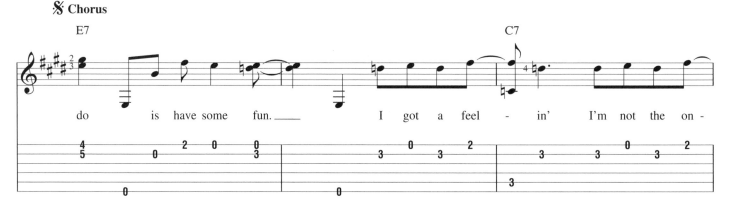

the record store, too.
one another.

Well, they're nothin' like Billy 'n' me. 'Cause all I wan-na
The bartender looks up from his want ads. But all I wan-na

% Chorus

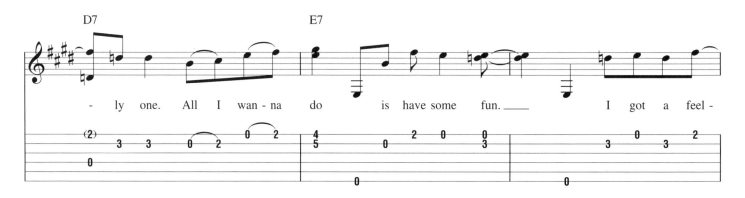

do is have some fun.___ I got a feel - in' I'm not the on-

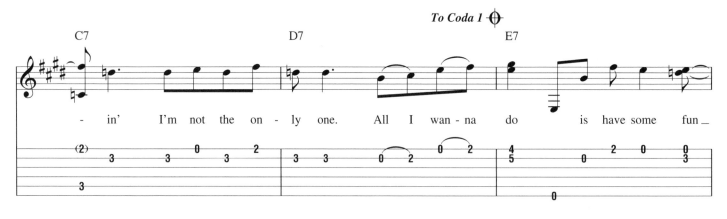

- ly one. All I wan-na do is have some fun.___ I got a feel -

To Coda 1 ⊕

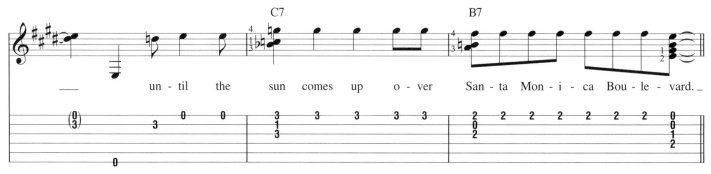

- in' I'm not the on - ly one. All I wan-na do is have some fun___

___ un - til the sun comes up o - ver San - ta Mon - i - ca Bou - le - vard.___

14

To Coda 2 ⊕ **Pre-Chorus**

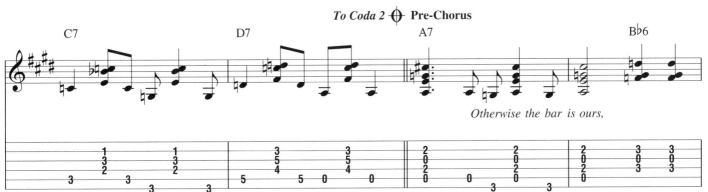

Otherwise the bar is ours,

the day and the night and the car wash, too. *The matches and the Buds and*

D.S. al Coda 1

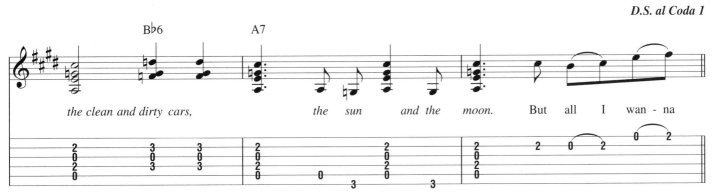

the clean and dirty cars, *the sun and the moon. But all I wan - na*

15

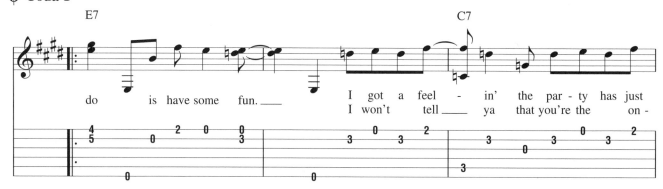

do   is   have   some   fun. ____   I   got   a   feel - in'   the   par - ty   has   just

I   won't   tell ____   ya   that   you're   the   on -

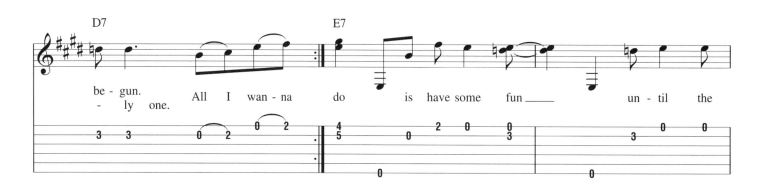

be - gun.   All   I   wan - na   do   is   have   some   fun ____   un - til   the

- ly   one.

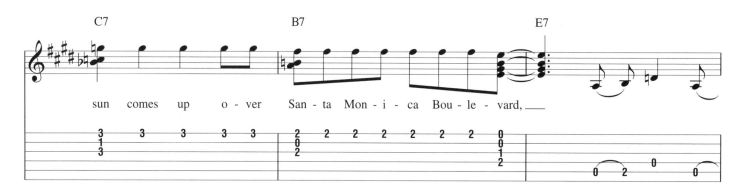

sun   comes   up   o - ver   San - ta   Mon - i - ca   Bou - le - vard, ____

D.S.S. al Coda 2
(no repeat)

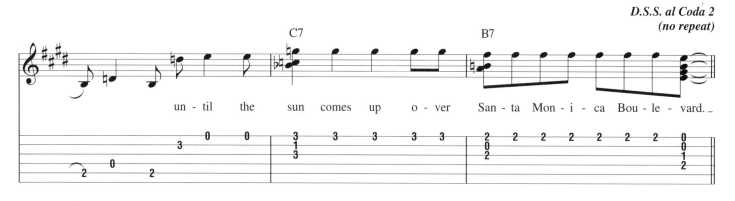

un - til   the   sun   comes   up   o - ver   San - ta   Mon - i - ca   Bou - le - vard. _

⊕ **Coda 2**

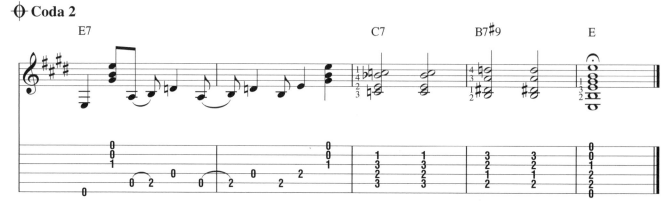

Beat It

Words and Music by Michael Jackson

Strum Pattern: 1, 2
Pick Pattern: 2, 4

Intro
Moderately fast

1. They told him, "Don't you ev - er come a - round here. Don't wan - na see your face; you bet - ter
2. *See additional lyrics*

dis - ap - pear." The fi - re's in their eyes and their words are real - ly clear. So

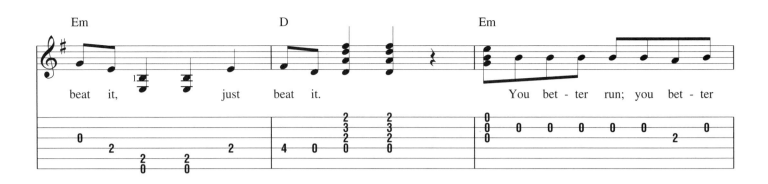

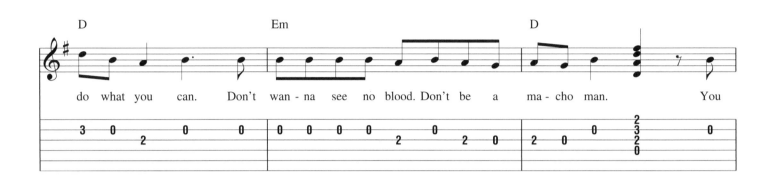

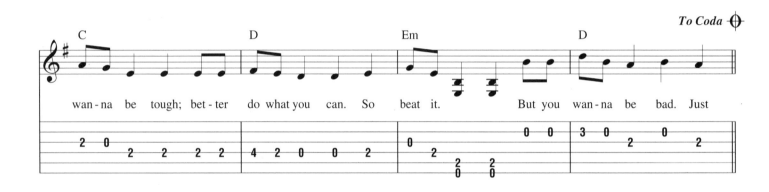

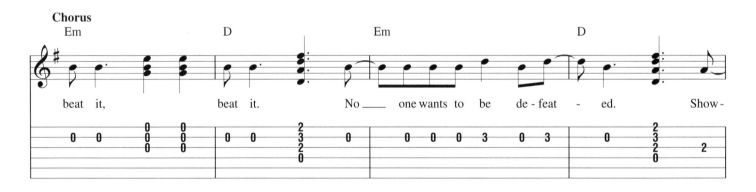

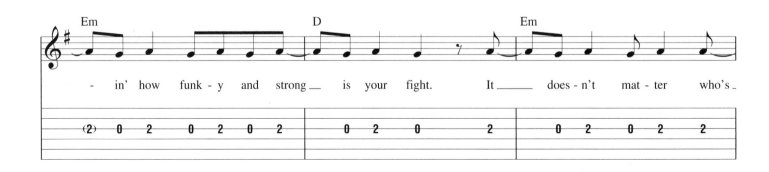

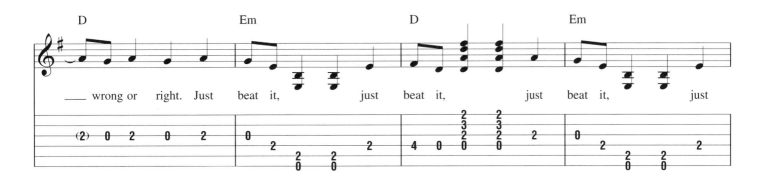

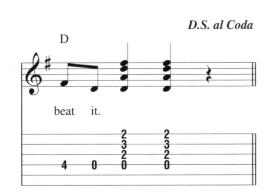

Coda

D.S. al Coda

Outro-Chorus

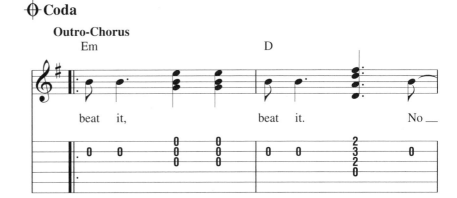

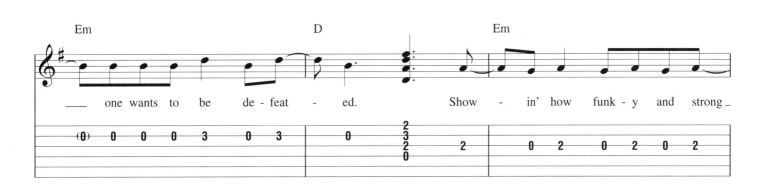

Repeat and fade

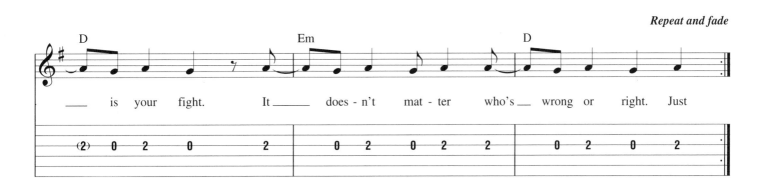

Additional Lyrics

2. They're out to get. Better leave while you can.
   Don't wanna be a bad boy; you wanna be a man.
   You wanna stay alive, better do what you can.
   So beat it, just beat it.
   You have to show them that you're not really scared.
   You're playin' with your life. This ain't no truth or dare.
   They'll kick you, then they beat you, then they'll tell you it's fair.
   So beat it. But you wanna be bad.

Another Day in Paradise

Words and Music by Phil Collins

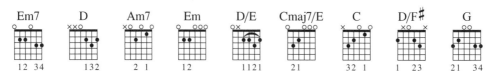

*Capo I

Strum Pattern: 3
Pick Pattern: 3

Intro
Moderately slow

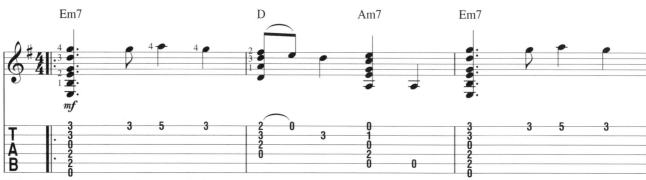

*Optional: To match recording, place capo at 1st fret.

Verse

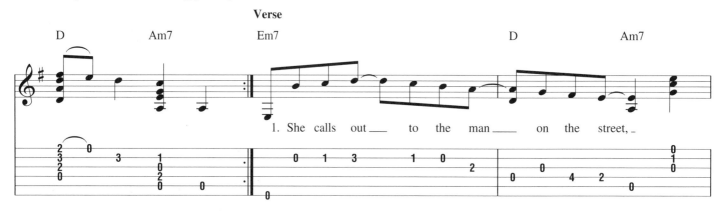

1. She calls out ___ to the man ___ on the street, ___

"Sir, ___ can you help ___ me?   It's cold ___ and I've no -

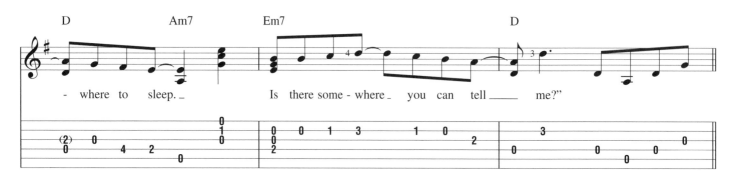

- where to sleep. ___   Is there some - where ___ you can tell ___ me?"

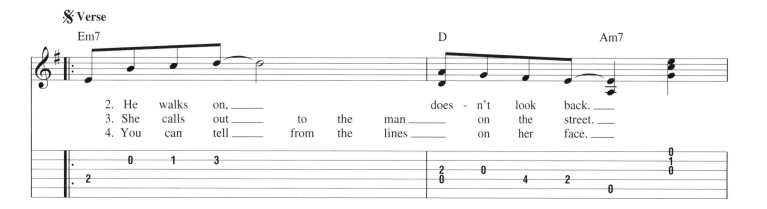

2. He walks on, _____ does - n't look back. _____
3. She calls out _____ to the man _____ on the street. _____
4. You can tell _____ from the lines _____ on her face. _____

He pre - tends _____ he can't hear _____ her.
He can see _____ she's been cry - ing.
You can see _____ that she's been _____ there.

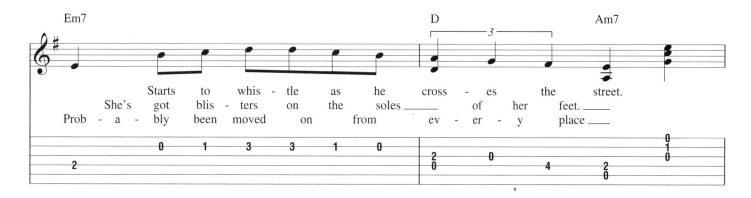

Starts to whis - tle as he cross - es the street.
She's got blis - ters on the soles _____ of her feet.
Prob - a - bly been moved on from ev - er - y place _____

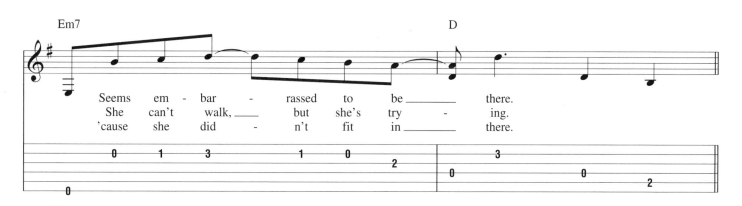

Seems em - bar - rassed to be _____ there.
She can't walk, _____ but she's try - ing.
'cause she did - n't fit in _____ there.

Chorus

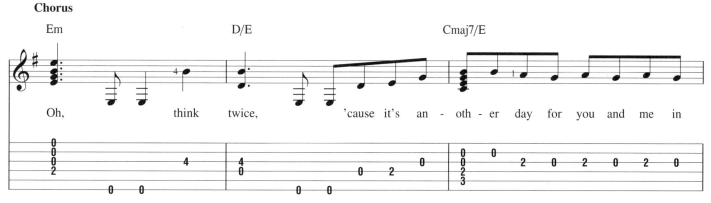

Oh, think twice, 'cause it's an - oth - er day for you and me in

Aquarius/Let the Sunshine In

from the Broadway Musical Production HAIR

Words by James Rado and Gerome Ragni
Music by Galt MacDermot

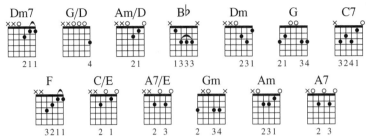

*Tune down 1 step:
(low to high) D-G-C-F-A-D

Strum Pattern: 4
Pick Pattern: 3

Intro
Very fast

*Optional: To match recording, tune down 1 step.

Verse

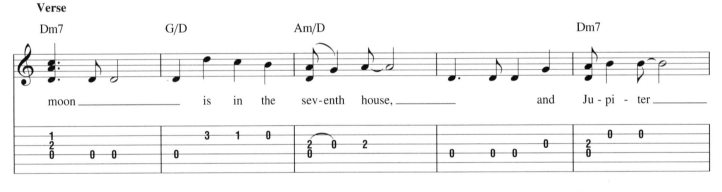

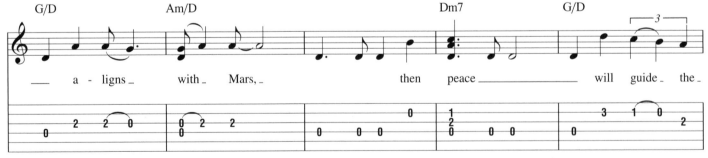

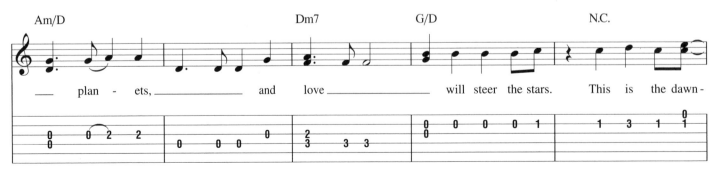

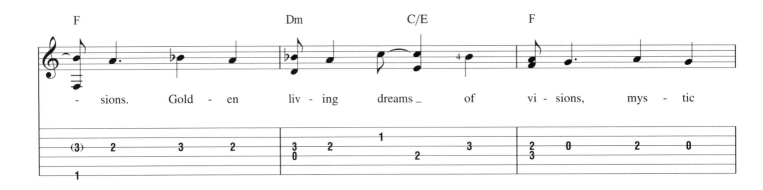

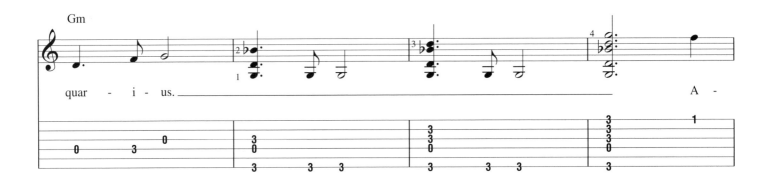

D.C. al Coda

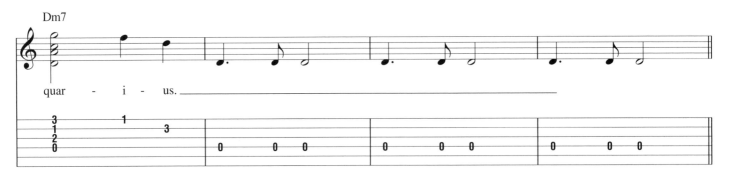

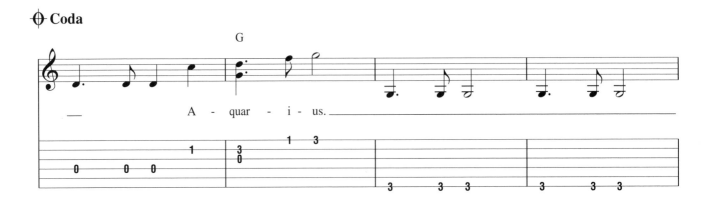

Dm7

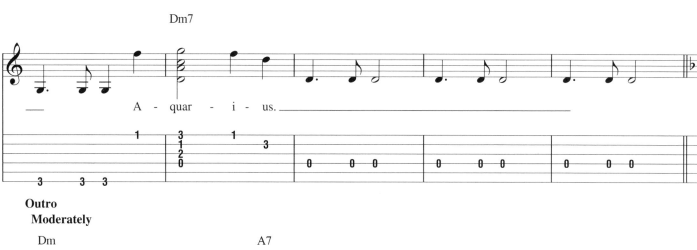

A - quar - i - us.

Outro
Moderately

Dm   A7

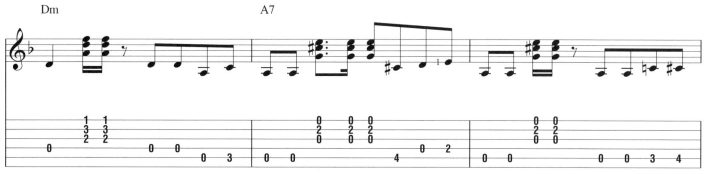

Dm   B♭   F

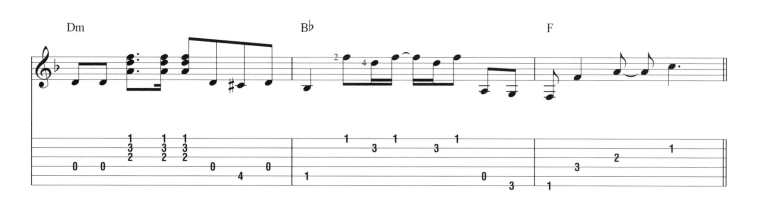

Dm   A7

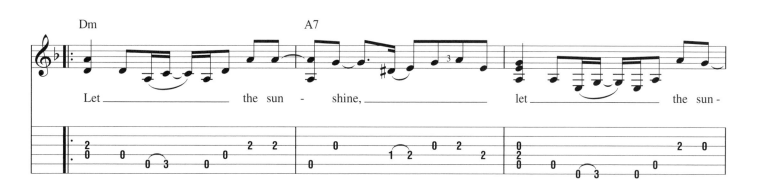

Let _____ the sun - shine, _____ let _____ the sun -

Repeat and fade

Dm   B♭   F

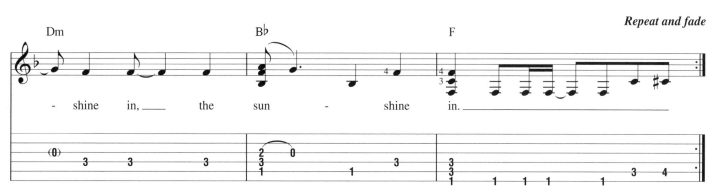

- shine in, ___ the sun - shine in. _____

Beautiful Day

Words by Bono
Music by U2

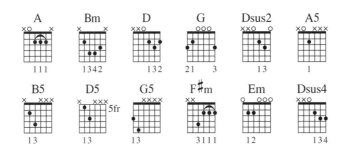

Strum Pattern: 1

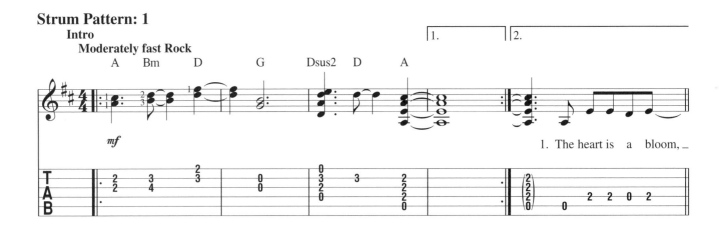

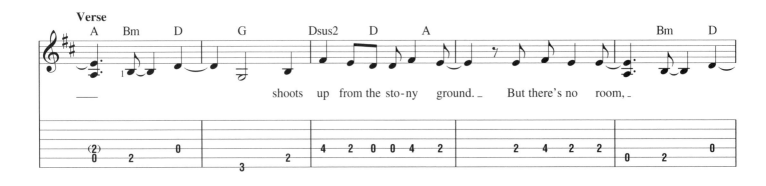

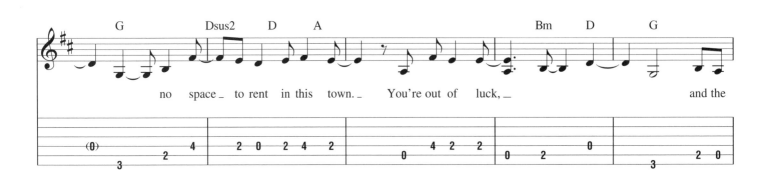

rea-son that you had to care. __ The traf-fic is stuck, __ and you're not

mov-ing an-y-where. You thought you'd found __ a friend __ to take you

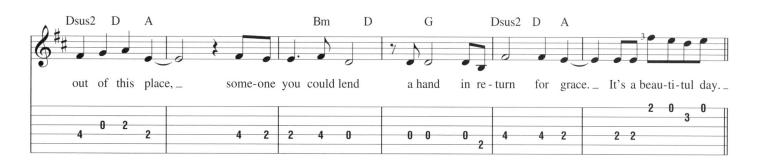

out of this place, __ some-one you could lend a hand in re-turn for grace. __ It's a beau-ti-tul day. __

Chorus

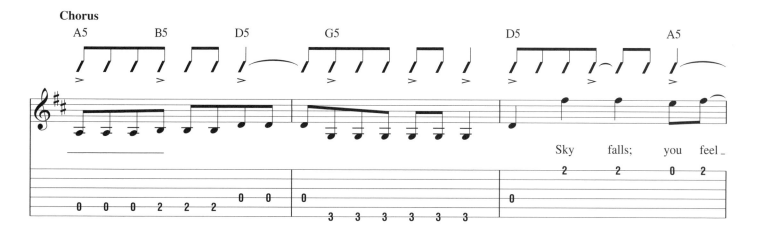

Sky falls; you feel __

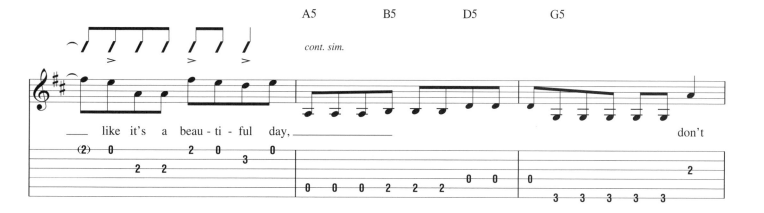

__ like it's a beau-ti-ful day, ___ don't

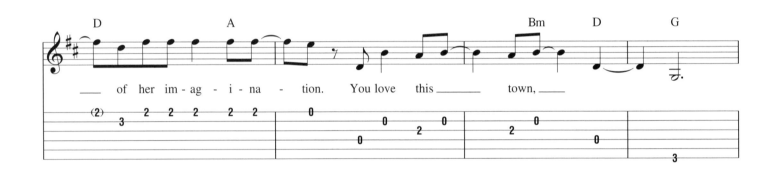

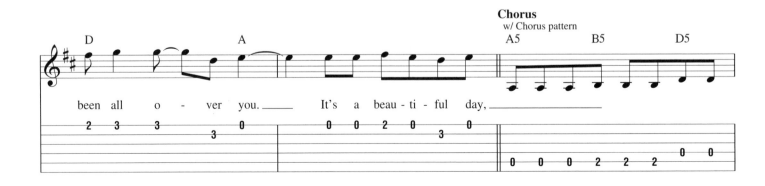

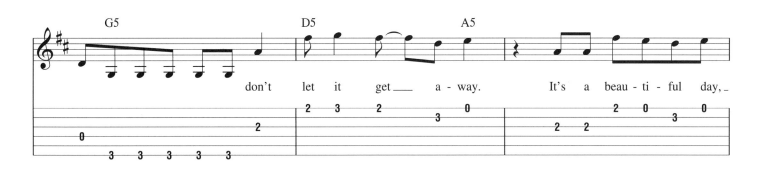

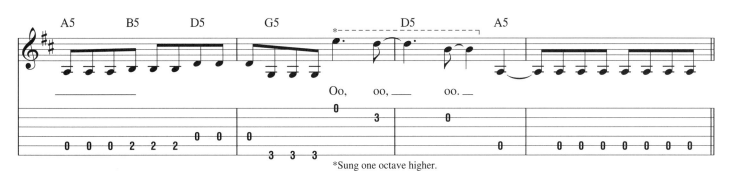

*Sung one octave higher.

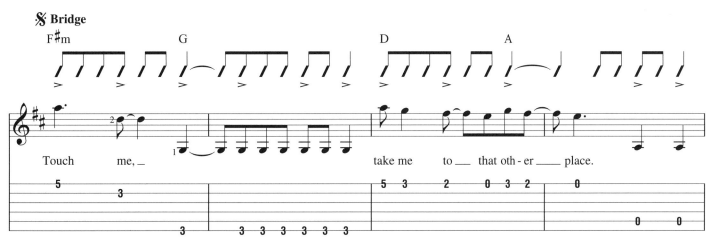

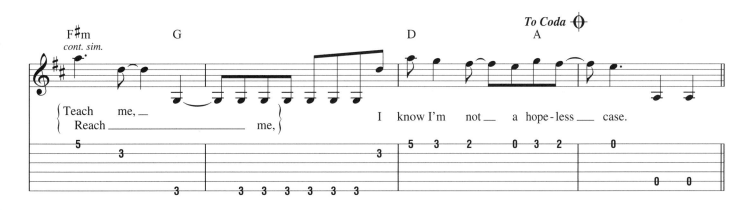

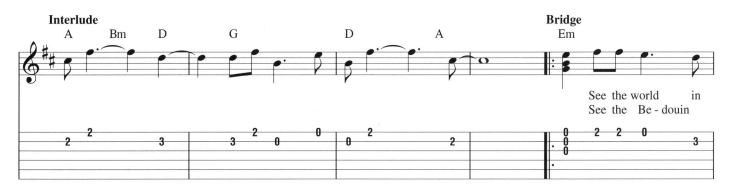

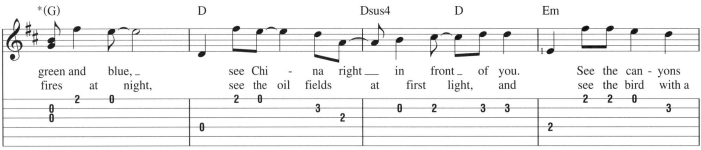

*(G)

green and blue, __ see Chi - na right __ in front __ of you. See the can - yons
fires at night, see the oil fields at first light, and see the bird with a

*Second time only.

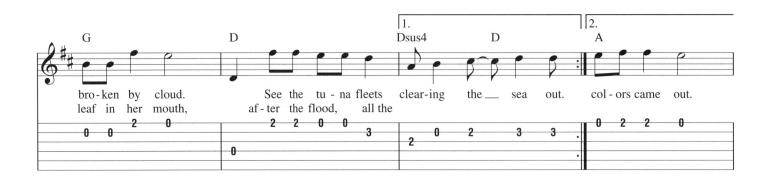

bro - ken by cloud. See the tu - na fleets clear-ing the __ sea out. col - ors came out.
leaf in her mouth, af - ter the flood, all the

Chorus
w/ Chorus pattern

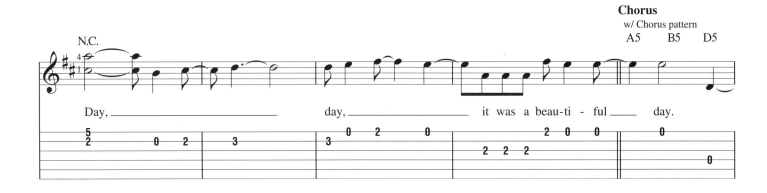

Day, _____ day, _____ it was a beau-ti - ful ___ day.

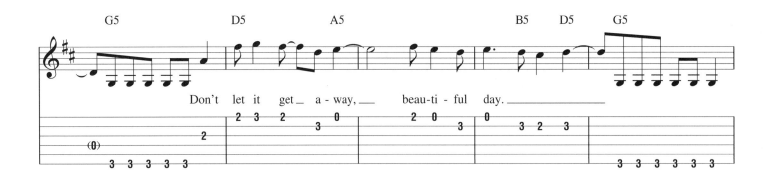

Don't let it get __ a - way, __ beau-ti - ful day. _____

D.S. al Coda

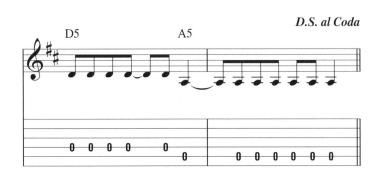

⊕ Coda

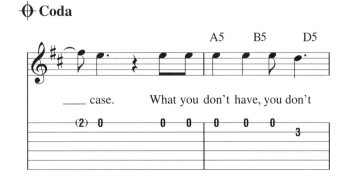

___ case. What you don't have, you don't

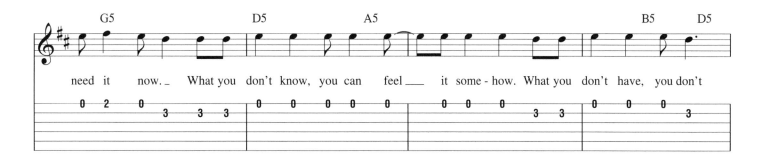

need it now._ What you don't know, you can feel __ it some - how. What you don't have, you don't

Outro-Chorus
w/ Chorus pattern

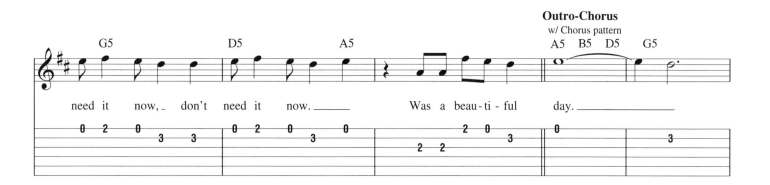

need it now,_ don't need it now._____ Was a beau-ti-ful day._____

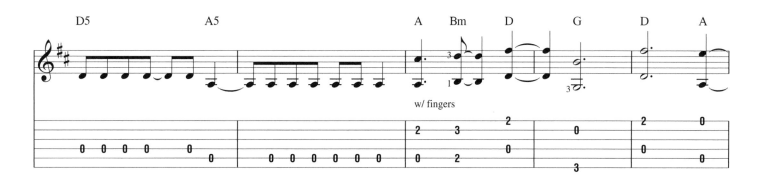

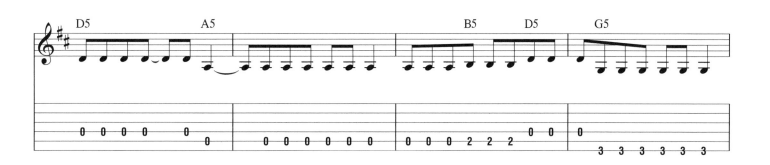

w/ fingers

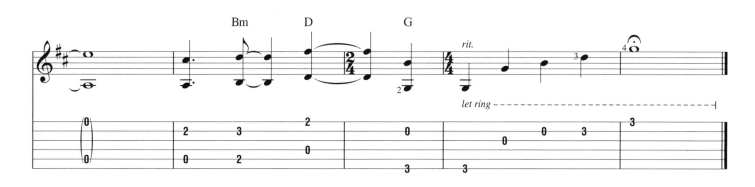

rit.

let ring -

33

Bette Davis Eyes

Words and Music by Donna Weiss and Jackie DeShannon

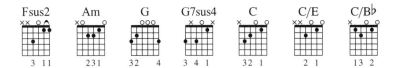

*Capo V

Strum Pattern: 2
Pick Pattern: 2

Intro
Moderately

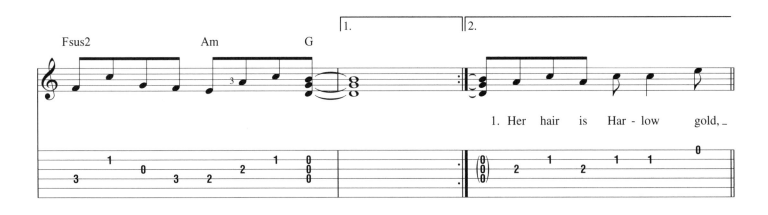

*Optional: To match recording, place capo at 5th fret.

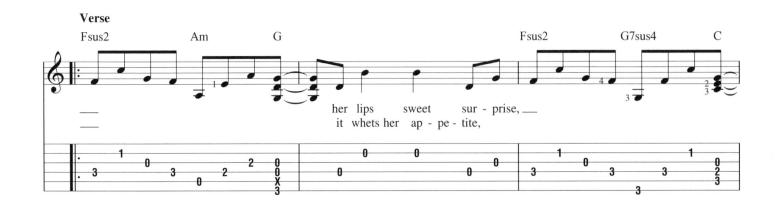

1. Her hair is Har-low gold, _

Verse

her lips   sweet   sur-prise, _
it whets her ap-pe-tite,

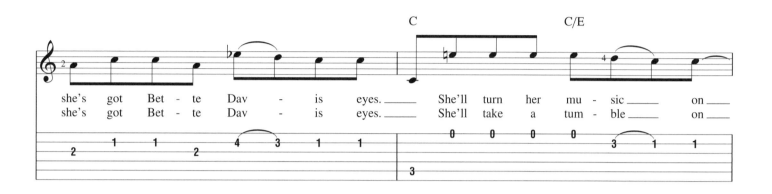

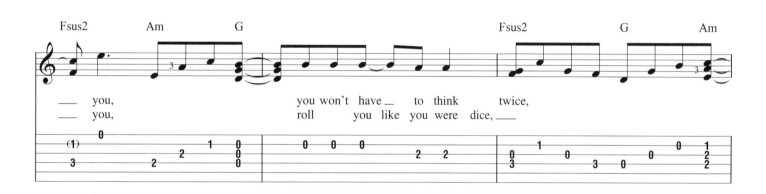

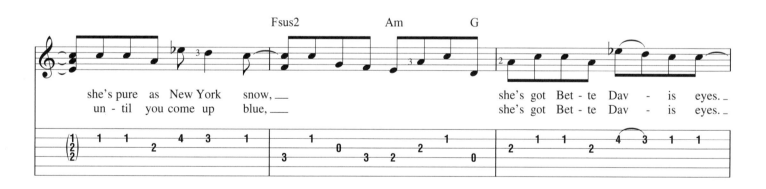

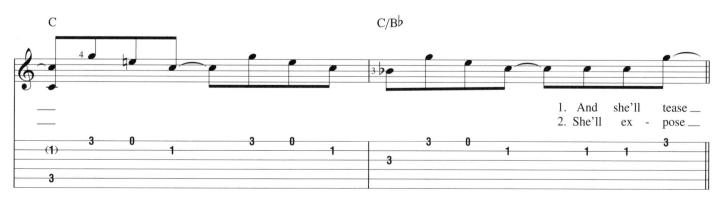

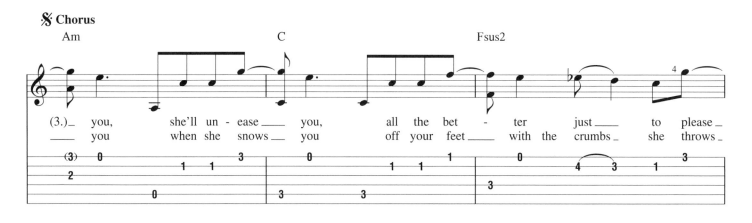

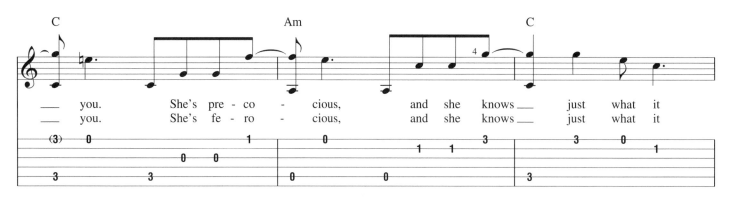

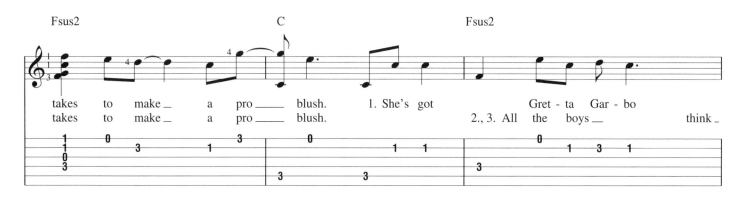

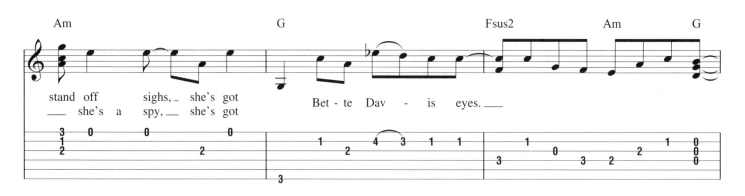

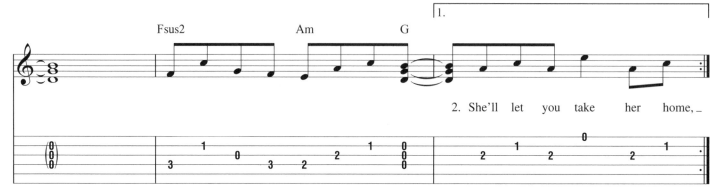

Boulevard of Broken Dreams

Words by Billie Joe
Music by Green Day

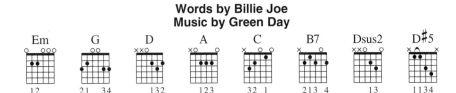

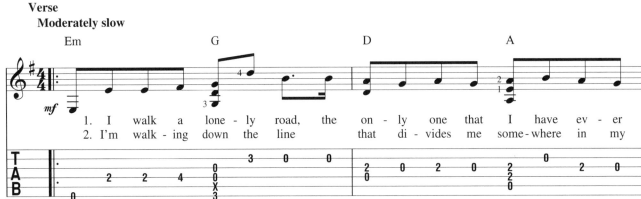

*Capo I

Strum Pattern: 3
Pick Pattern: 3

Verse
Moderately slow

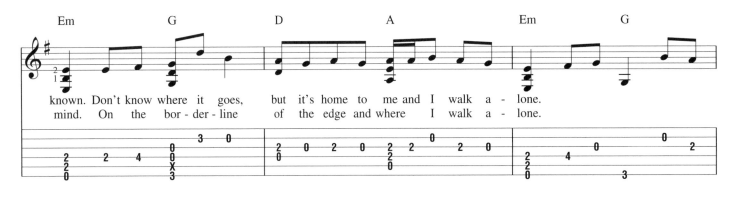

1. I walk a lone-ly road, the on-ly one that I have ev-er
2. I'm walk-ing down the line that di-vides me some-where in my

*Optional: To match recording, place capo at 1st fret.

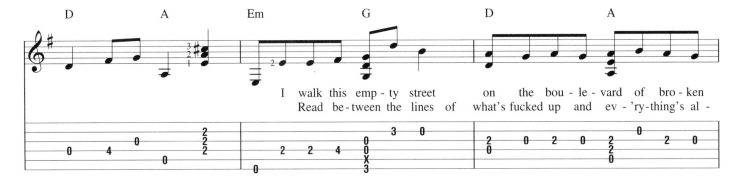

known. Don't know where it goes, but it's home to me and I walk a - lone.
mind. On the bor-der - line of the edge and where I walk a - lone.

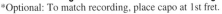

I walk this emp-ty street on the bou-le-vard of bro-ken
Read be-tween the lines of what's fucked up and ev-'ry-thing's al -

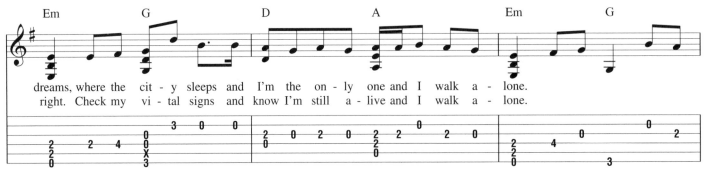

dreams, where the cit-y sleeps and I'm the on-ly one and I walk a - lone.
right. Check my vi-tal signs and know I'm still a - live and I walk a - lone.

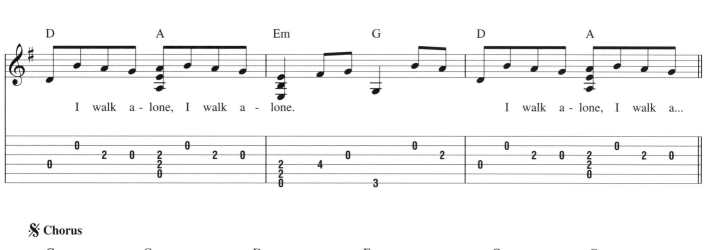

I walk a - lone, I walk a - lone.   I walk a - lone, I walk a...

𝄋 Chorus

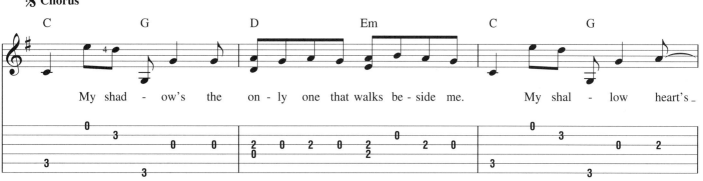

My shad - ow's the on - ly one that walks be - side me.   My shal - low heart's _

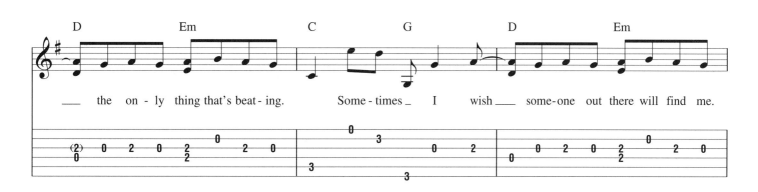

_ the on - ly thing that's beat - ing.   Some - times _ I wish _ some-one out there will find me.

To Coda ⊕   **Interlude**

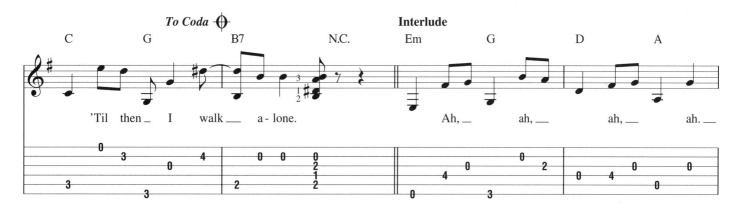

'Til then _ I walk _ a - lone.   Ah, _ ah, _ ah, _ ah. _

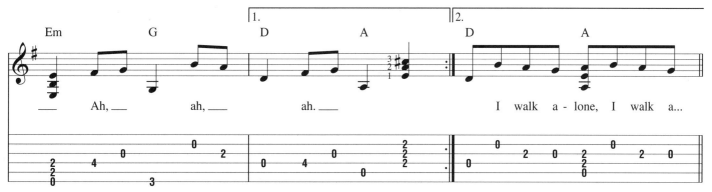

_ Ah, _ ah, _ ah. _   I walk a - lone, I walk a...

Clocks

Words and Music by Guy Berryman, Jon Buckland, Will Champion and Chris Martin

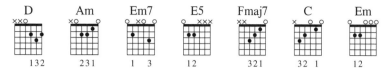

Strum Pattern: 1, 5
Pick Pattern: 2, 4

Intro
Moderately fast

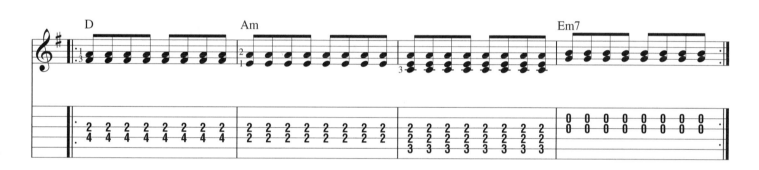

Verse

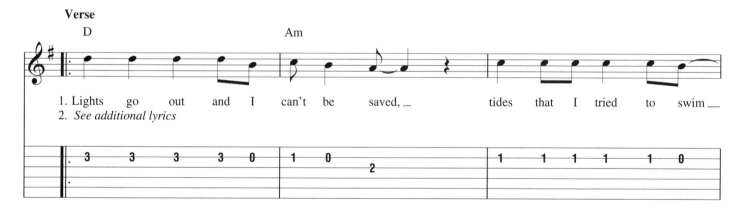

1. Lights go out and I can't be saved, ___ tides that I tried to swim ___
2. *See additional lyrics*

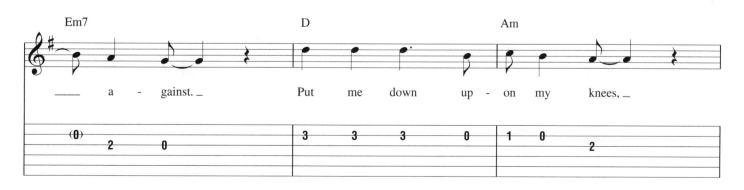

___ a - gainst. ___ Put me down up - on my knees, ___

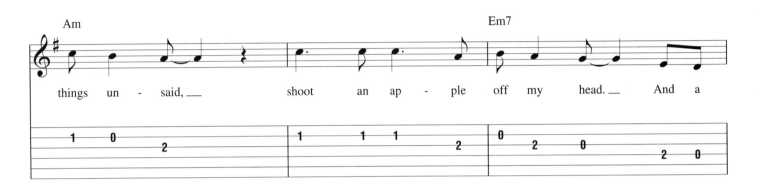

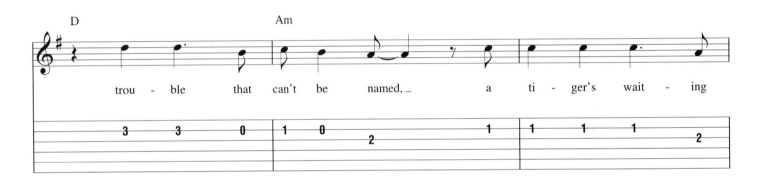

Chorus

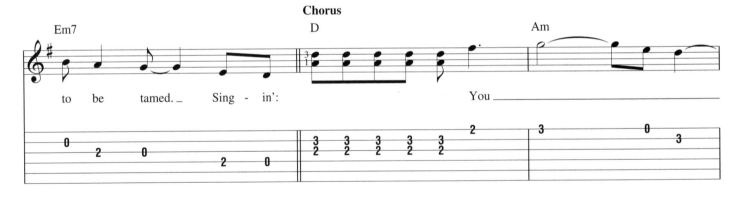

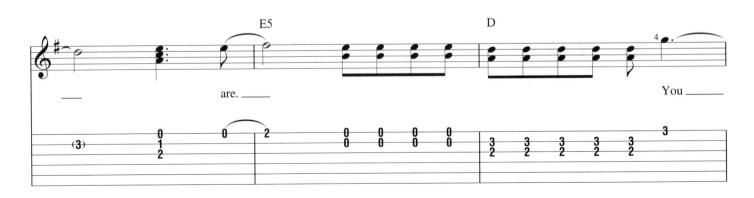

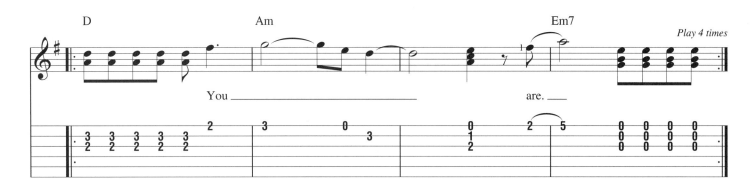

Play 4 times

You _____ are. ___

Bridge

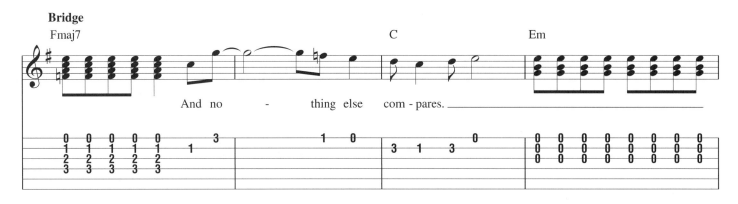

And no - thing else com - pares. _____

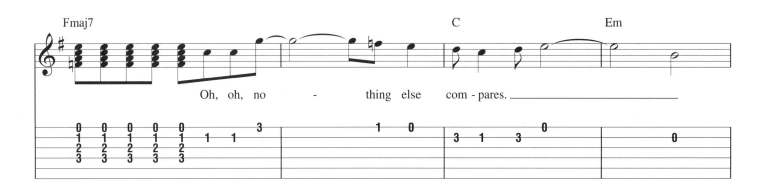

Oh, oh, no - thing else com - pares. _____

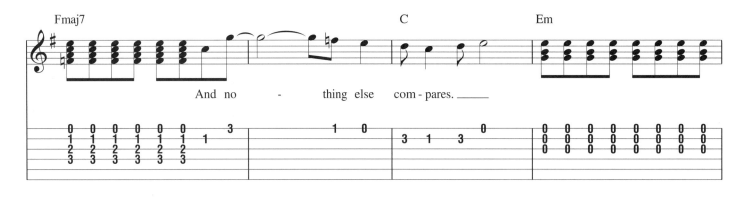

And no - thing else com - pares. ___

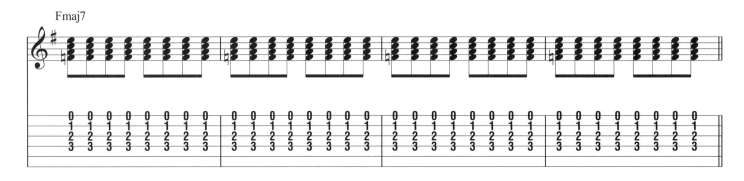

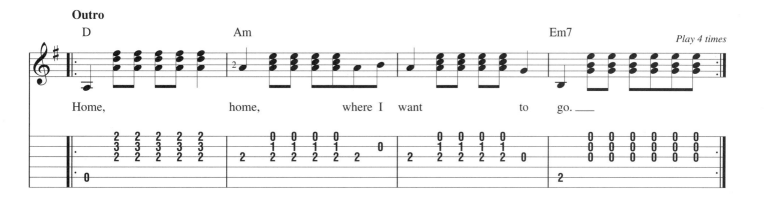

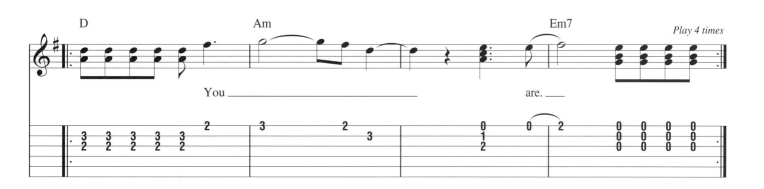

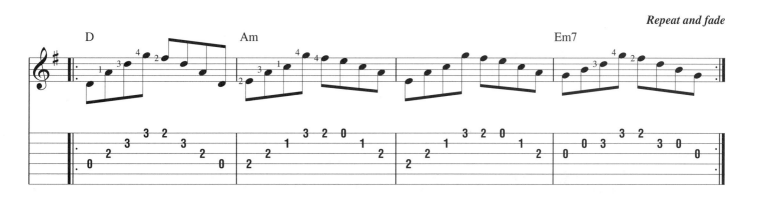

Additional Lyrics

2. Confusion that never stops, closing walls and tickin' clocks.
   Gonna come back and take you home, I could not stop, that you now know.
   Singin': come out upon my seas, cursed missed opportunities.
   Am I a part of the cure, or am I part of the disease?

Bridge Over Troubled Water

Words and Music by Paul Simon

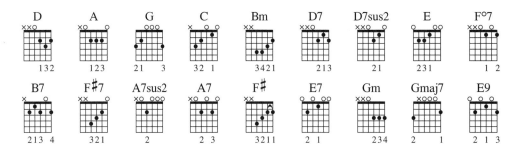

Strum Pattern: 3
Pick Pattern: 4

Intro
Moderately

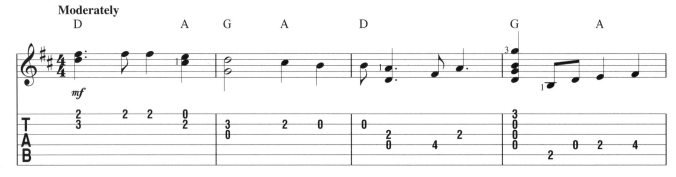

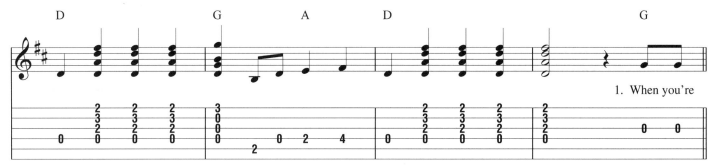

1. When you're

Verse

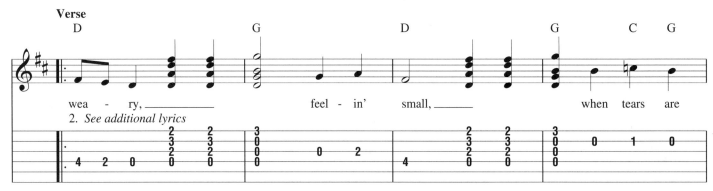

wea - ry, _____ feel - in' small, _____ when tears are

2. See additional lyrics

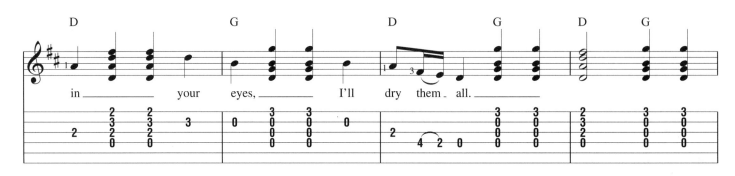

in _____ your eyes, _____ I'll dry them _ all. _____

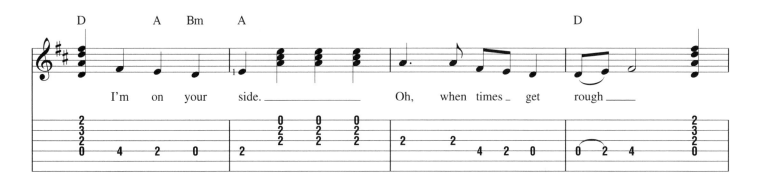

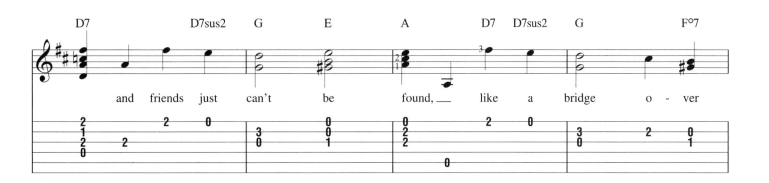

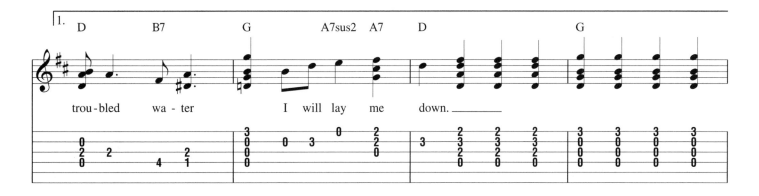

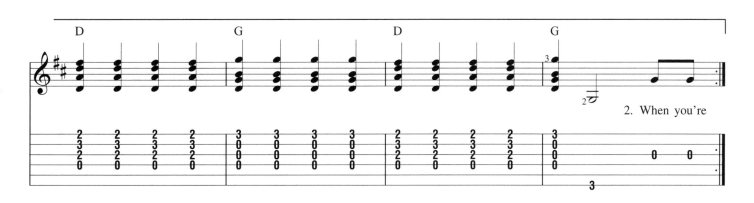

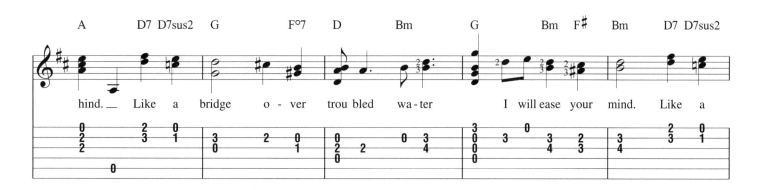

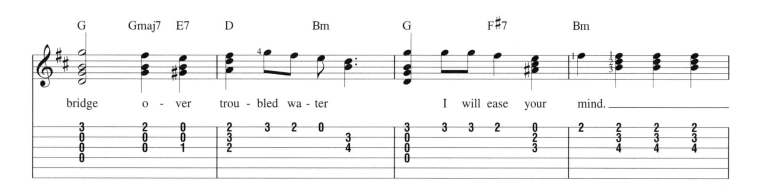

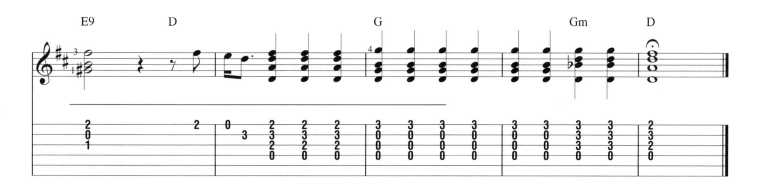

Additional Lyrics

2. When you're down and out,
   When you're on the street,
   When evening falls so hard
   I will comfort you,
   I'll take your part.
   Oh, when darkness comes
   And pain is all around,
   Like a bridge over troubled water
   I will lay me down.
   Like a bridge over troubled water
   I will lay me down.

Change the World

Words and Music by Wayne Kirkpatrick, Gordon Kennedy and Tommy Sims

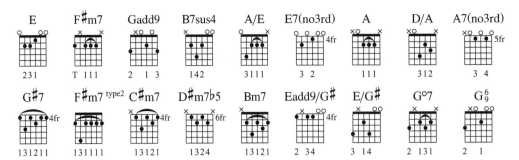

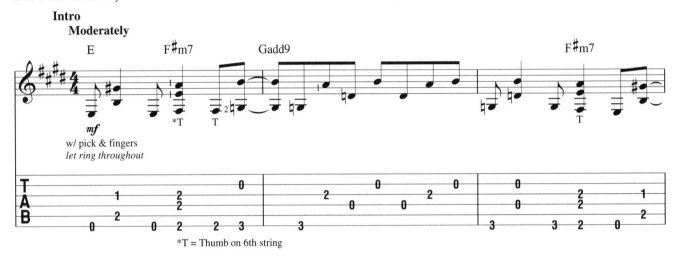

Strum Pattern: 2, 3
Pick Pattern: 3, 4

Intro
Moderately

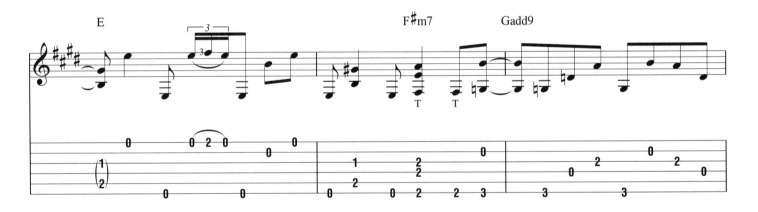

*T = Thumb on 6th string

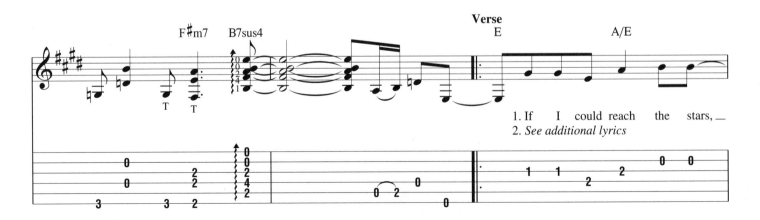

1. If I could reach the stars, __
2. *See additional lyrics*

51

u - ni - verse. ___ You would think ___ my love was real - ly some - thing good, ___ ba - by

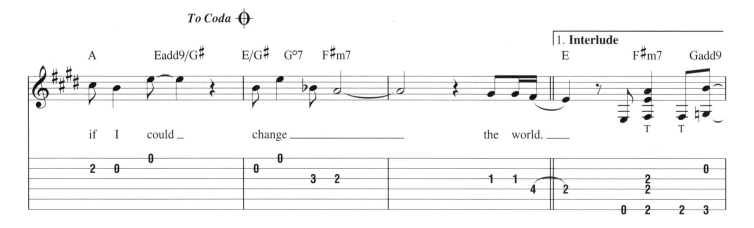

To Coda ⊕

if I could ___ change ___ the world. ___

1. **Interlude**

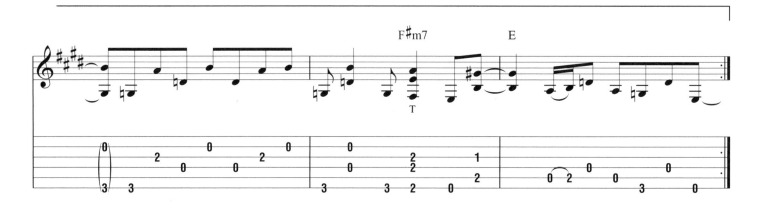

2. **Guitar Solo**

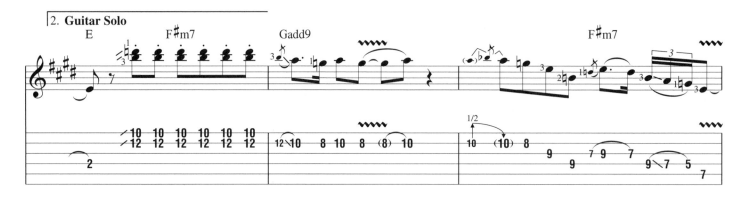

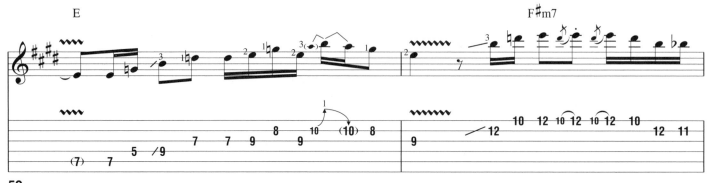

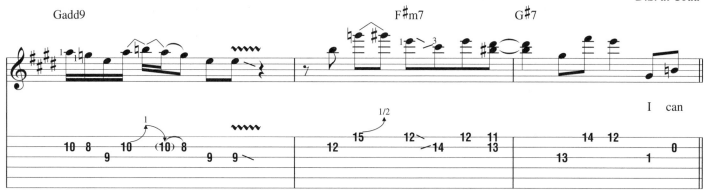

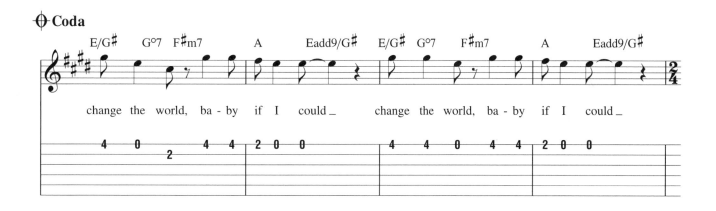

Additional Lyrics

2. If I could be king, even for a day,
   I'd take you as my queen, I'd have it no other way.
   And our love would rule in this kingdom we have made.
   Till then I'd be a fool, wishing for the day.

Days of Wine and Roses

Lyrics by Johnny Mercer
Music by Henry Mancini

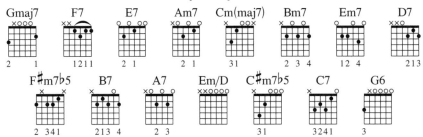

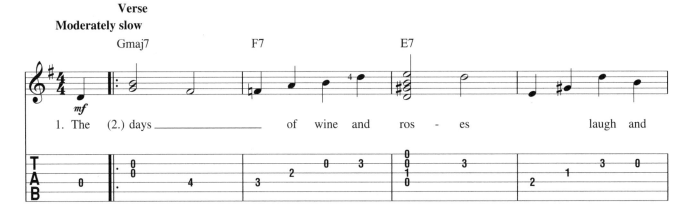

Strum Pattern: 3
Pick Pattern: 3

Verse
Moderately slow

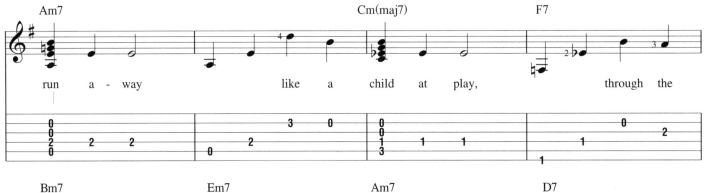

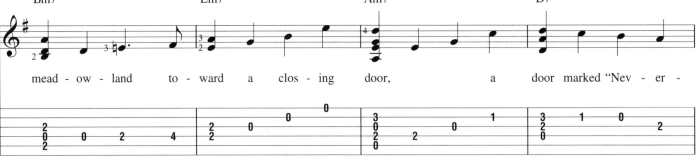

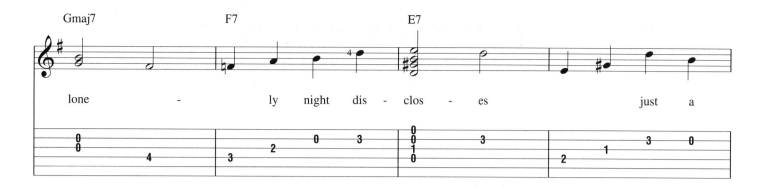

lone - ly night dis - clos - es just a

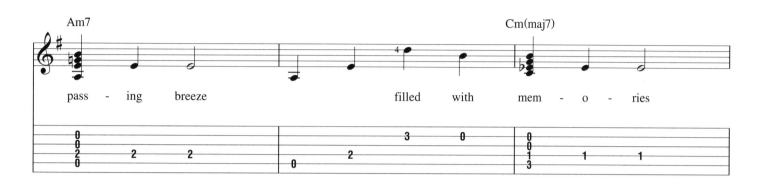

pass - ing breeze filled with mem - o - ries

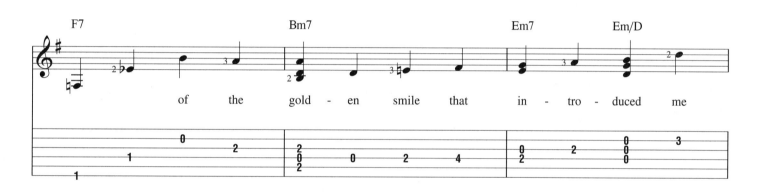

of the gold - en smile that in - tro - duced me

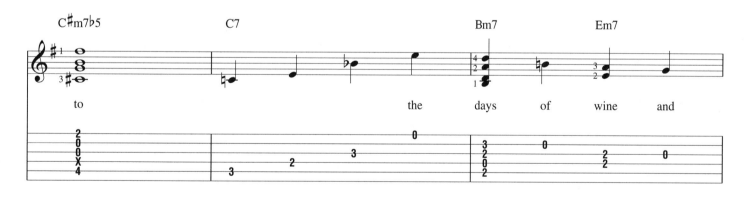

to the days of wine and

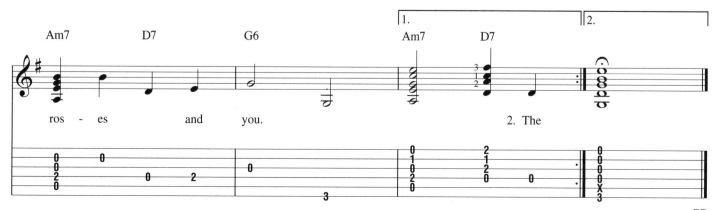

ros - es and you. 2. The

Don't Know Why

Words and Music by Jesse Harris

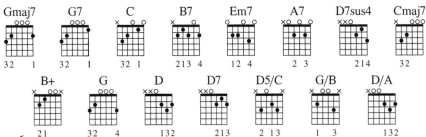

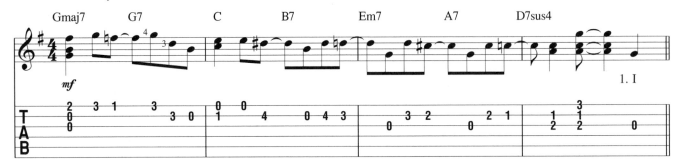

Strum Pattern: 6
Pick Pattern: 4

Intro
Moderately slow

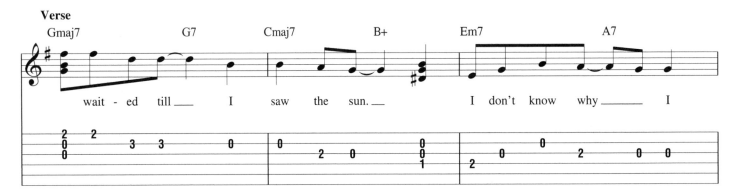

Verse

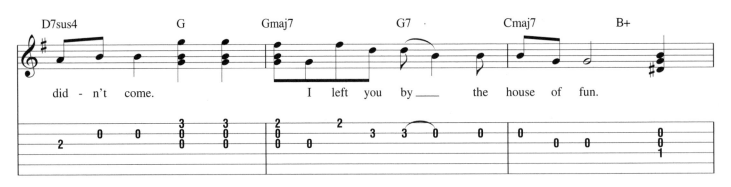

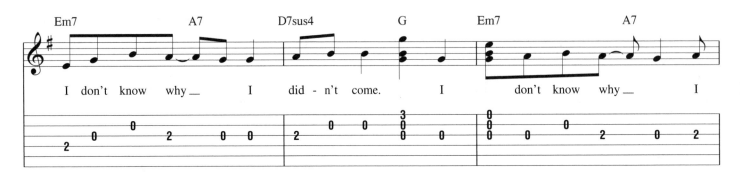

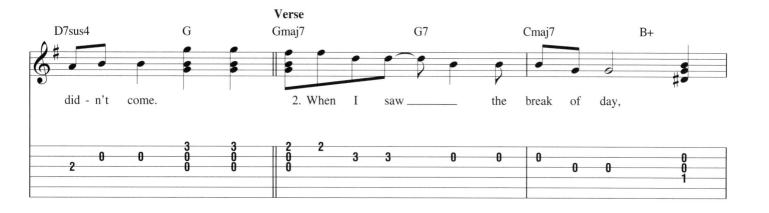

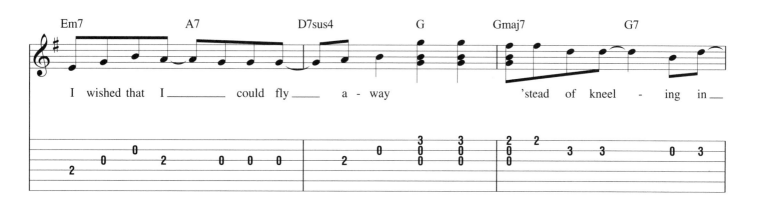

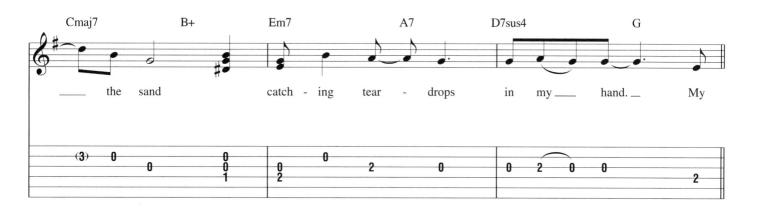

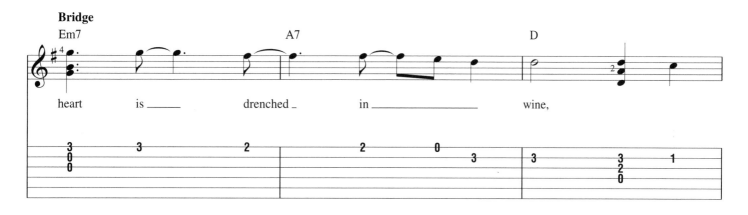

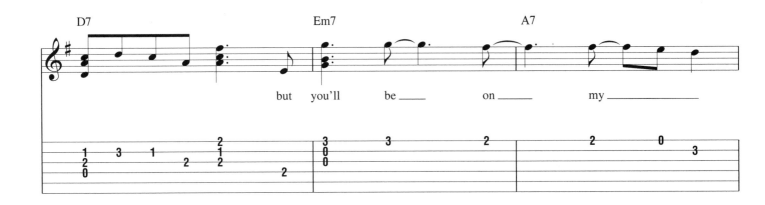

but you'll be _____ on _____ my _____

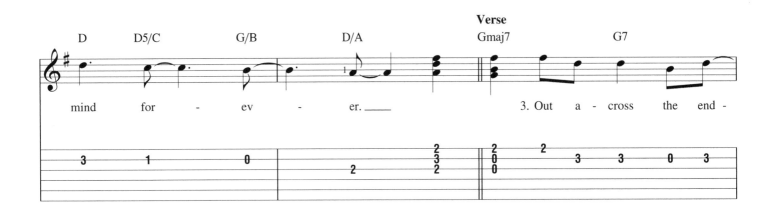

Verse

mind for - ev - er. _____ 3. Out a - cross the end -

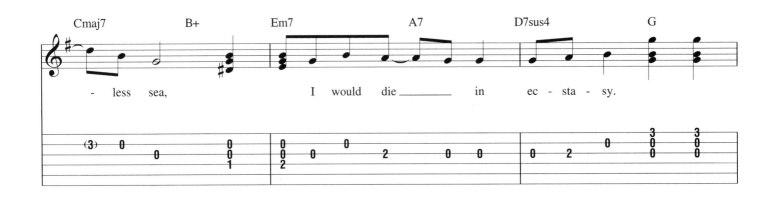

- less sea, I would die _____ in ec - sta - sy.

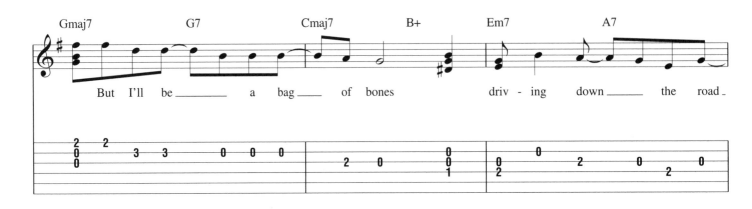

But I'll be _____ a bag ___ of bones driv - ing down _____ the road _

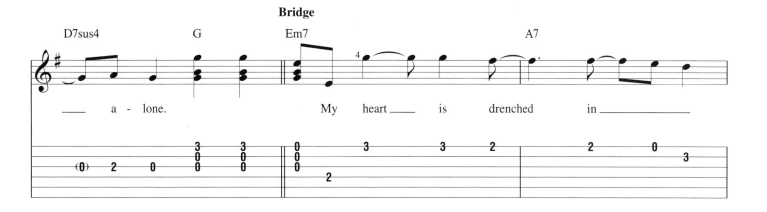

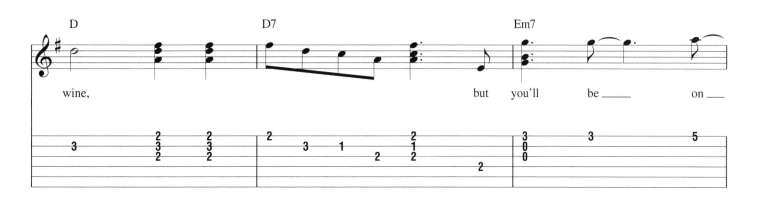

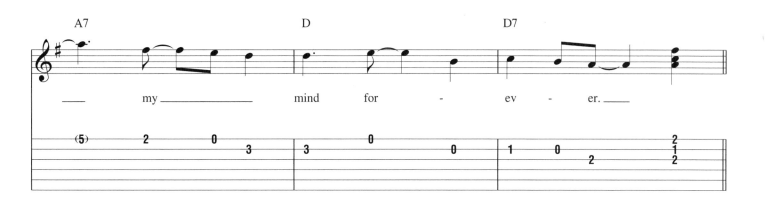

Interlude

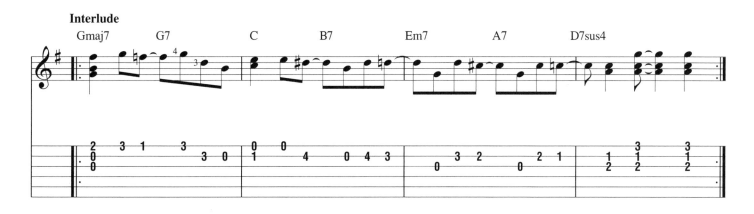

Outro-Verse

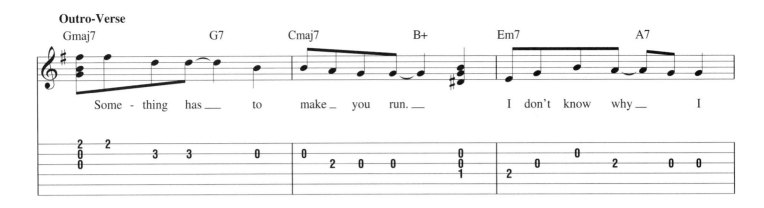

Some - thing has __ to make _ you run. __ I don't know why __ I

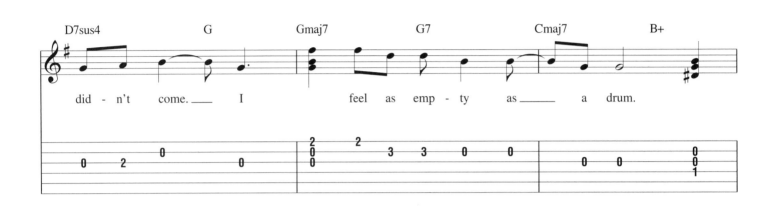

did - n't come. ___ I feel as emp - ty as _____ a drum.

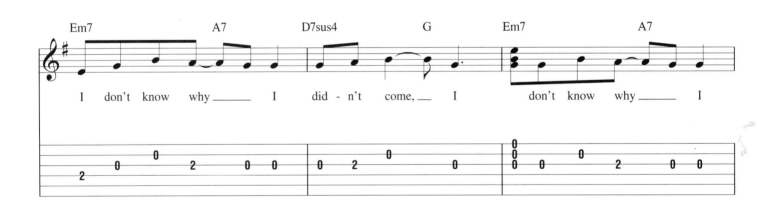

I don't know why _____ I did - n't come, __ I don't know why _____ I

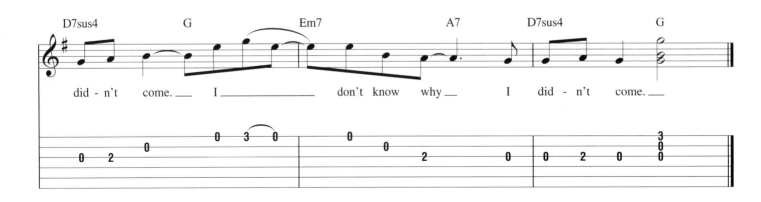

did - n't come. __ I _____ don't know why _ I did - n't come. __

Don't Worry, Be Happy

Words and Music by Bobby McFerrin

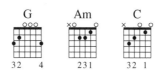

*Capo IV

Strum Pattern: 3
Pick Pattern: 3

Intro
Moderately fast

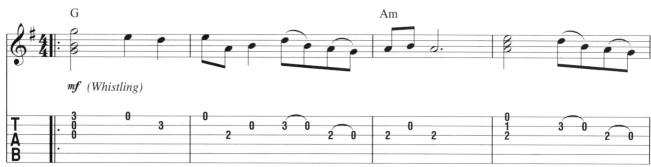

(Whistling)

*Optional: To match recording, place capo at 4th fret.

Verse

1. Here's a lit-tle song I wrote. ___ You might want to sing it note ___
2. Ain't got no place to lay ___ your head. ___ Some-bod-y came and took ___
3. Ain't got no cash, ain't got ___ no style. ___ Ain't ___ got no gal to make ___
4. *See additional lyrics*

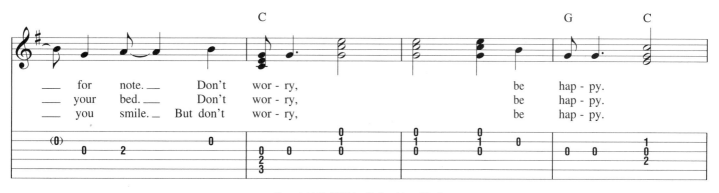

___ for note. ___ Don't wor-ry, be hap-py.
___ your bed. ___ Don't wor-ry, be hap-py.
___ you smile. ___ But don't wor-ry, be hap-py.

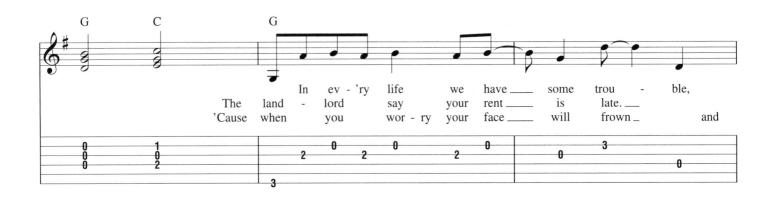

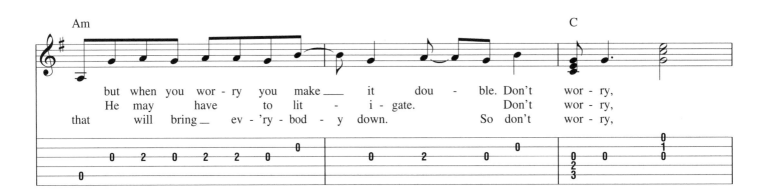

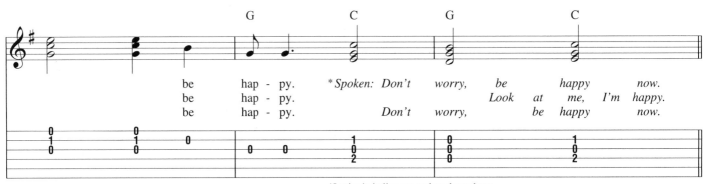

*Lyrics in italics are spoken throughout.

Chorus

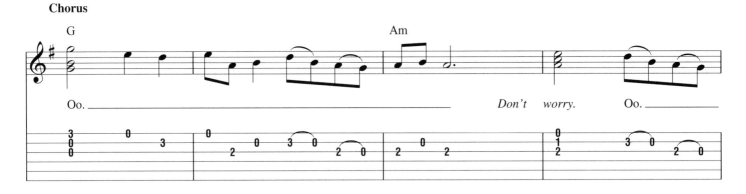

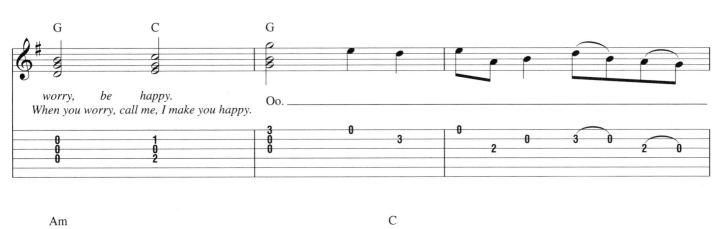

worry, be happy.
When you worry, call me, I make you happy.

Oo. _____

_____ Don't worry. Oo. _____ Be happy. Oo. _____

1., 2., 3.

_____ Don't worry, be happy.

4.

_____ Don't wor-ry, be hap-py.

Outro-Chorus
w/ Lead Voc. ad lib.

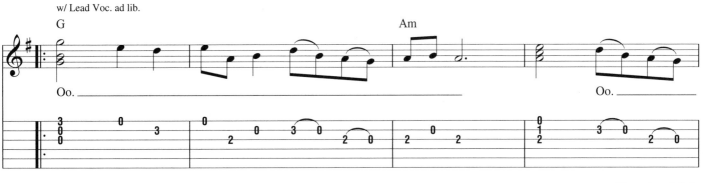

Oo. _____

Oo. _____

Repeat and fade

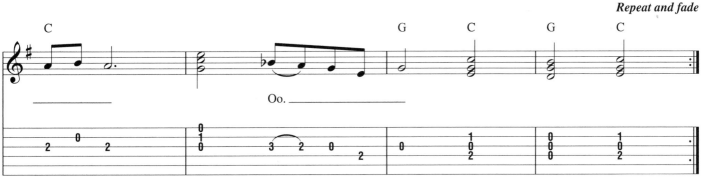

_____ Oo. _____

Additional Lyrics

4. *Now there is this song I wrote,*
   I hope you learned it note for note like good little children,
   Don't worry, be happy.
   Listen to what I say: in your life, expect some trouble,
   But when you worry you make it double,
   Don't worry, be happy, be happy now.

The First Time Ever I Saw Your Face

Words and Music by Ewan MacColl

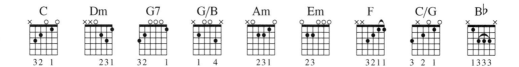

Strum Pattern: 3
Pick Pattern: 5

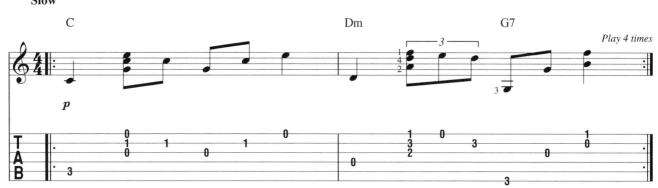

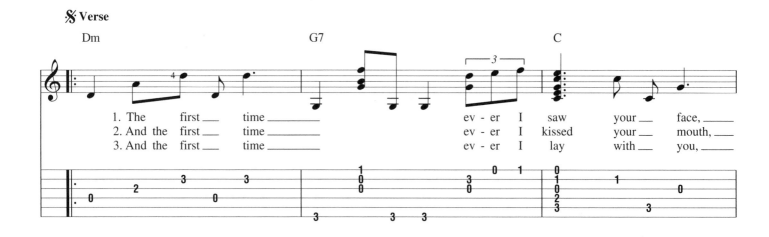

Coda

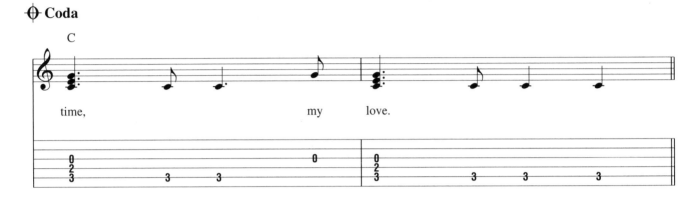

Outro

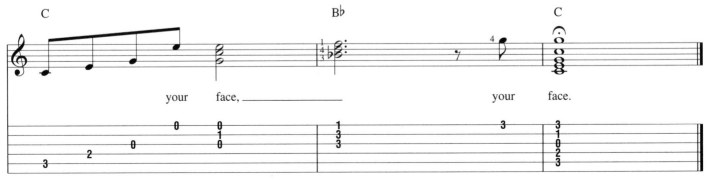

The Girl from Ipanema

(Garôta de Ipanema)

Music by Antonio Carlos Jobim
English Words by Norman Gimbel
Original Words by Vinicius de Moraes

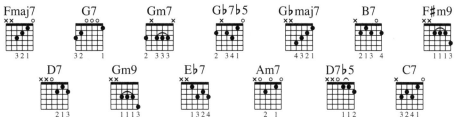

Strum Pattern: 3
Pick Pattern: 3

Verse
Moderate Bossa Nova

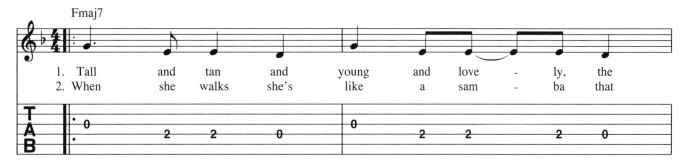

1. Tall and tan and young and love - ly, the
2. When she walks she's like a sam - ba that

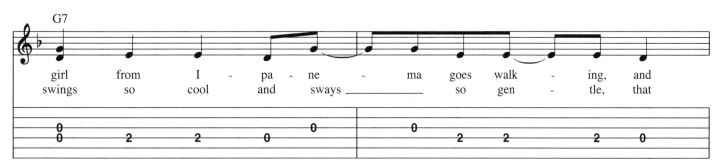

girl from I - pa - ne - ma goes walk - ing, and
swings so cool and sways _____ so gen - tle, that

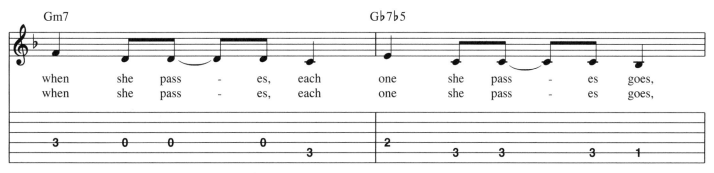

when she pass - es, each one she pass - es goes,
when she pass - es, each one she pass - es goes,

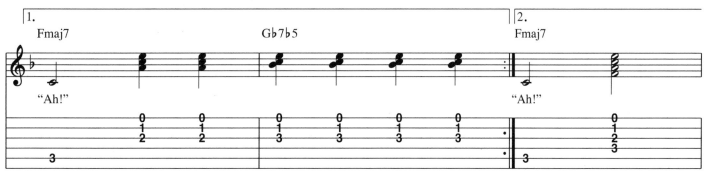

1.
Fmaj7   Gb7b5
"Ah!"

2.
Fmaj7
"Ah!"

Bridge

Graceland

Words and Music by Paul Simon

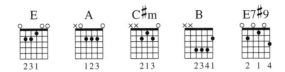

Strum Pattern: 6
Pick Pattern: 5

Intro
Moderately

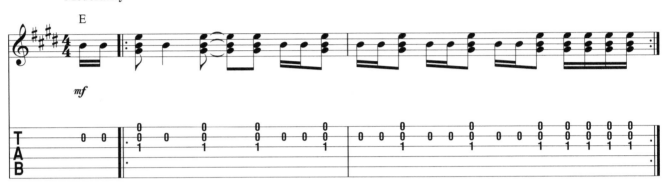

Verse

1. The Mis-sis-sip-pi Del-ta was shin-ing like a Na-tion-al ___ gui-tar.

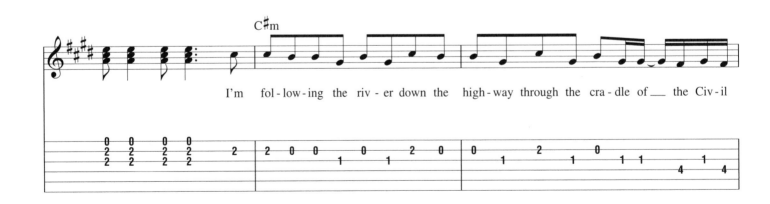

I'm fol-low-ing the riv-er down the high-way through the cra-dle of ___ the Civ-il

I've rea-son to be-lieve we {both / all} will be re-ceived (in

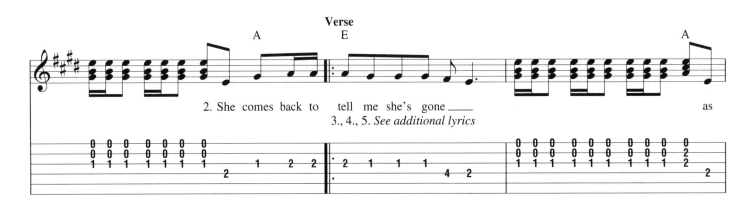

Grace-land.

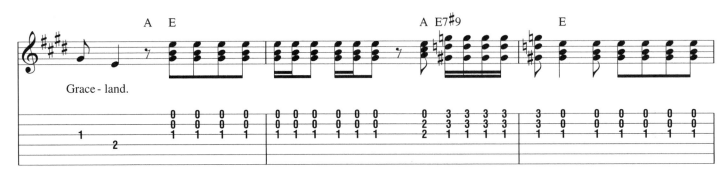

Verse

2. She comes back to tell me she's gone _____
3., 4., 5. *See additional lyrics*

as

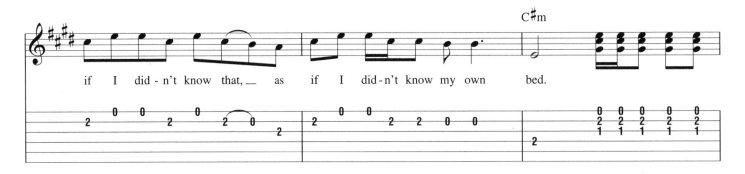

if I did-n't know that, __ as if I did-n't know my own bed.

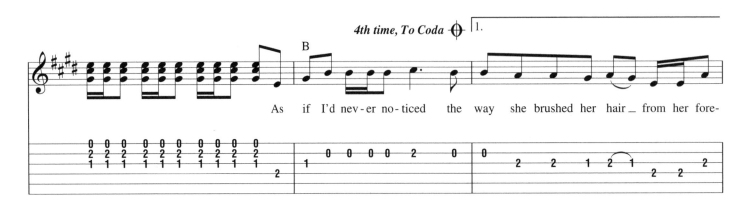

4th time, To Coda

As if I'd nev-er no-ticed the way she brushed her hair __ from her fore-

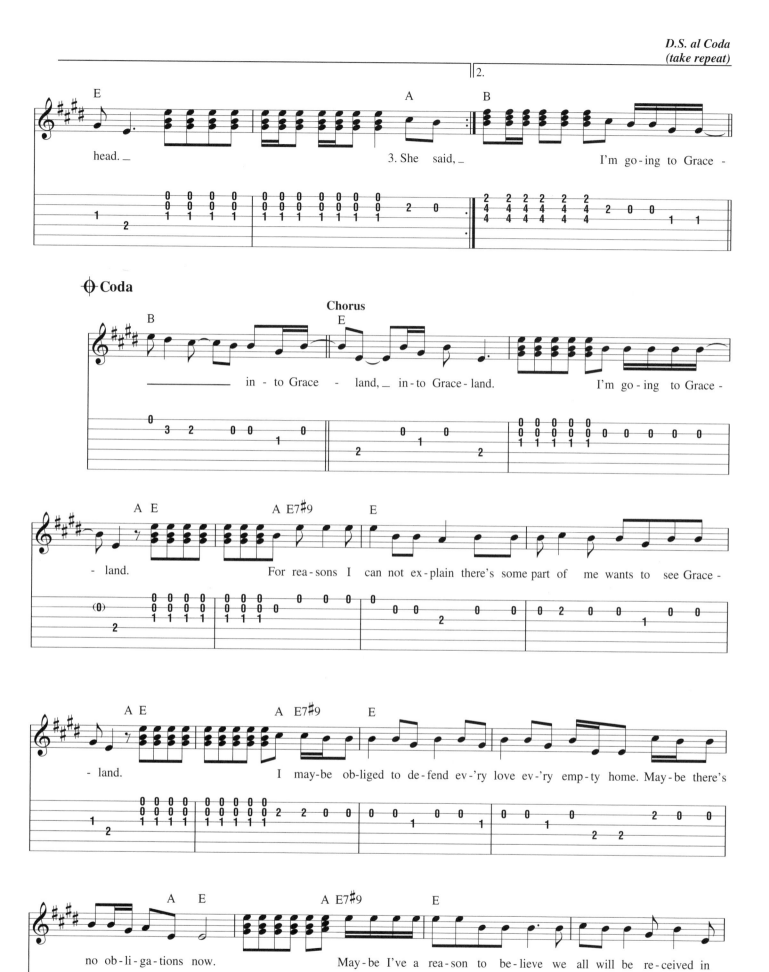

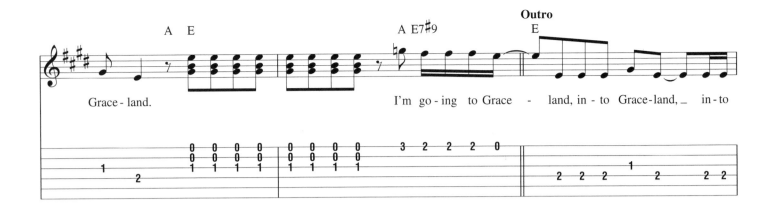

Grace - land.   I'm go - ing to Grace - land, in - to Grace-land, __ in - to

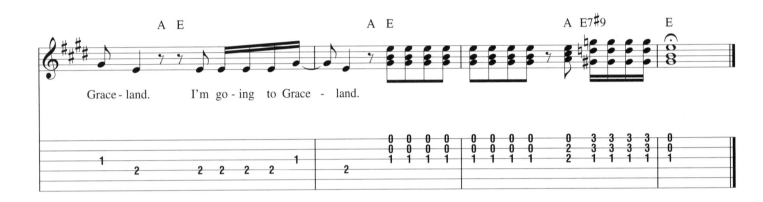

Grace - land.   I'm go - ing to Grace - land.

Additional Lyrics

3. She said, losing love
   Is like a window in your heart,
   And ev'rybody sees you're blown apart.
   Ev'rybody feels the wind blow.

4. There's a girl in New York City
   Who calls herself the human trampoline.
   Sometimes when I'm falling, flying,
   Tumbling in turmoil I say,
   "Oh, this is what she means.
   She means we are bouncing into Graceland."

5. And I see losing love
   Is like a window in your heart,
   And ev'rybody sees you're blown apart.
   Ev'rybody feels the wind blow.

Hotel California

Words and Music by Don Henley, Glenn Frey and Don Felder

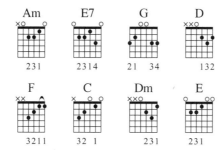

Strum Pattern: 3
Pick Pattern: 4

Intro
Moderate Rock, in 2

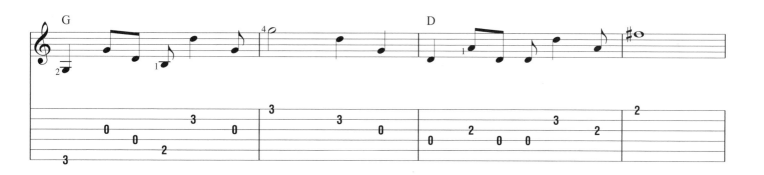

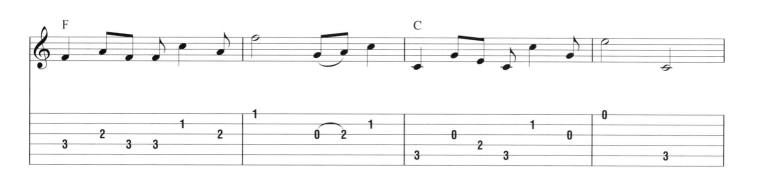

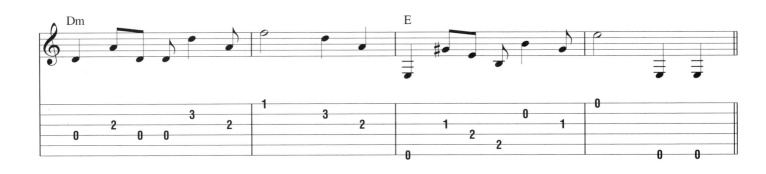

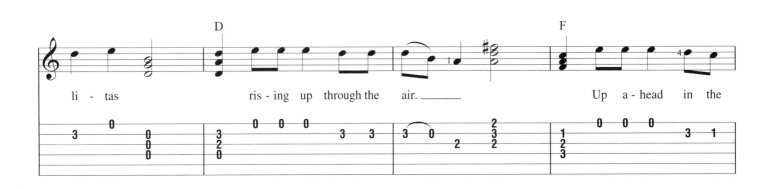

door - way; I heard the mis - sion bell. ___ And I was think-ing

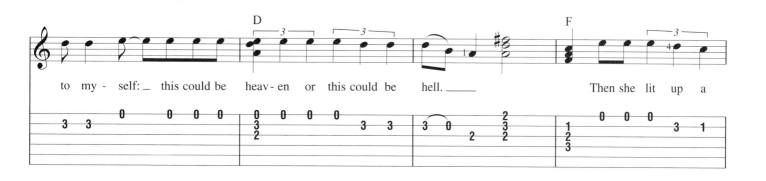

to my - self: __ this could be heav - en or this could be hell. _____ Then she lit up a

can - dle, and she showed me the way. There were voic-es down the

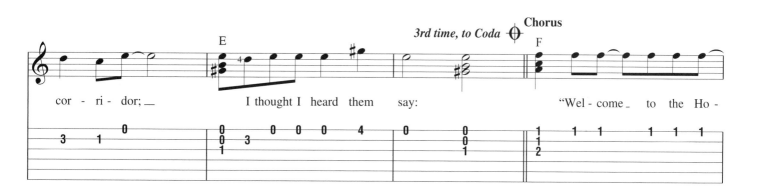

cor - ri - dor; __ I thought I heard them say: "Wel - come _ to the Ho -

- tel Cal - i - for - nia. Such a love - ly place,_ (Such a

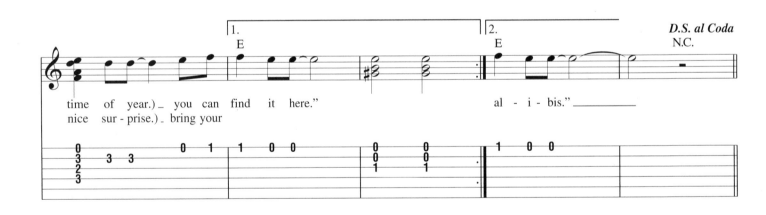

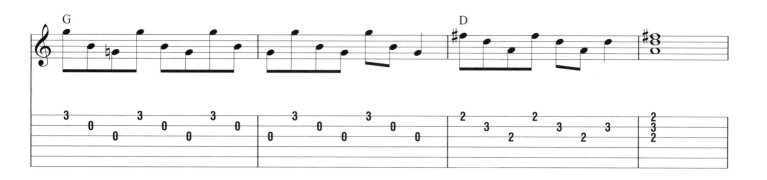

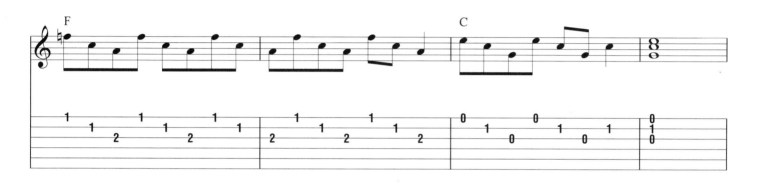

Repeat and fade

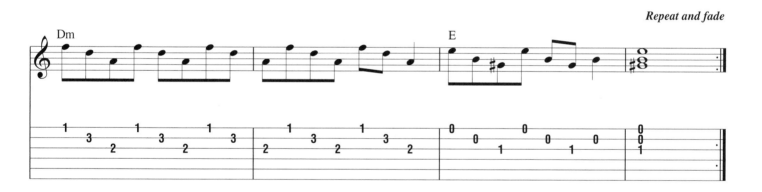

Additional Lyrics

2. Her mind is Tiffany twisted. She got the Mercedes bends.
   She got a lot of pretty, pretty boys that she calls friends.
   How they dance in the courtyard; sweet summer sweat.
   Some dance to remember; some dance to forget.
   So I called up the captain: "Please bring me my wine."
   He said, "We haven't had that spirit here since nineteen sixty-nine."
   And still those voices are calling from far away;
   Wake you up in the middle of the night just to hear them say:

3. Mirrors on the ceiling, the pink champagne on ice,
   And she said, "We are all just prisoners here of our own device."
   And in the master's chambers, they gathered for the feast.
   They stab it with their steely knives, but they just can't kill the beast.
   Last thing I remember, I was running for the door.
   I had to find the passage back to the place I was before.
   "Relax," said the night man. "We are programmed to receive.
   You can check out any time you like, but you can never leave."

Here We Go Again

Words and Music by Red Steagall and Donnie Lanier

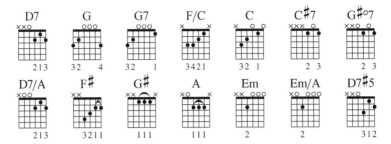

*Capo III

Strum Pattern: 1
Pick Pattern: 5

*Optional: To match recording, place capo at 3rd fret.

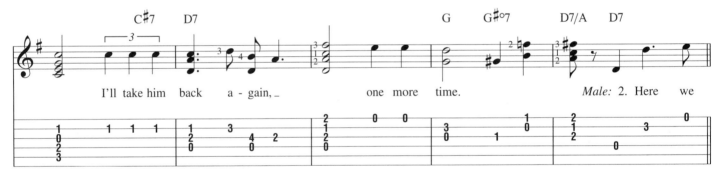

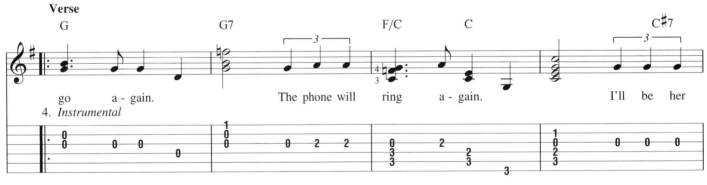

Higher Love

Words and Music by Will Jennings and Steve Winwood

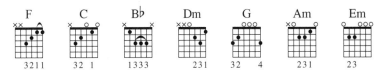

*Capo V

Strum Pattern: 6
Pick Pattern: 6

Verse

Moderately

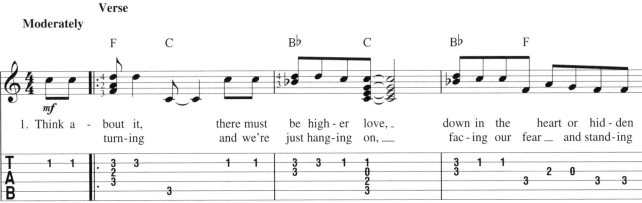

1. Think a-bout it, there must be high-er love, down in the heart or hid-den
turn-ing and we're just hang-ing on, fac-ing our fear and stand-ing

*Optional: To match recording, place capo at 5th fret.

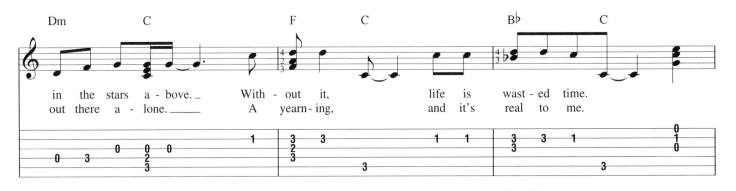

in the stars a-bove. With-out it, life is wast-ed time.
out there a-lone. A yearn-ing, and it's real to me.

Pre-Chorus

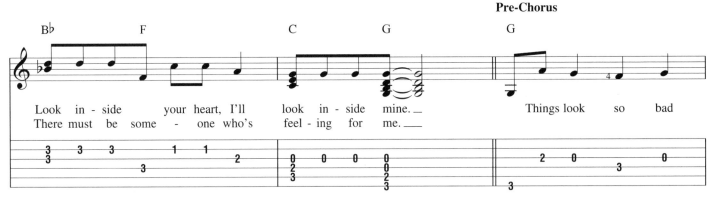

Look in-side your heart, I'll look in-side mine. Things look so bad
There must be some - one who's feel-ing for me.

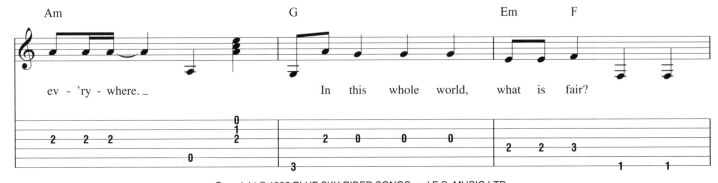

ev-'ry-where. In this whole world, what is fair?

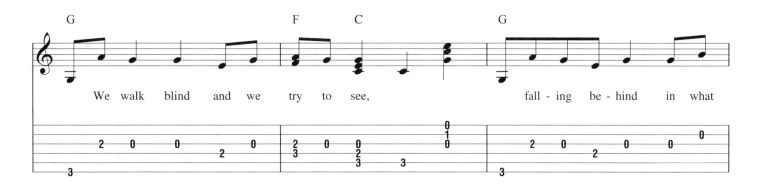

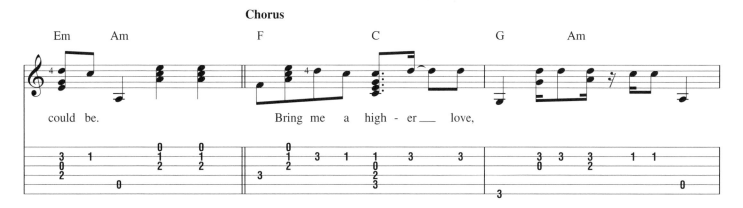

Chorus

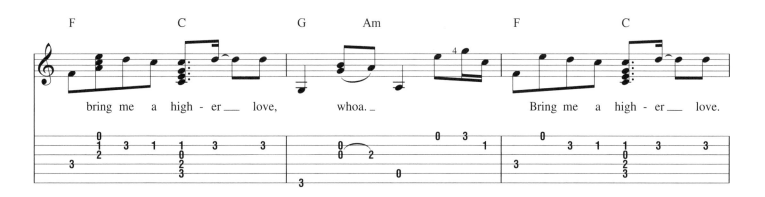

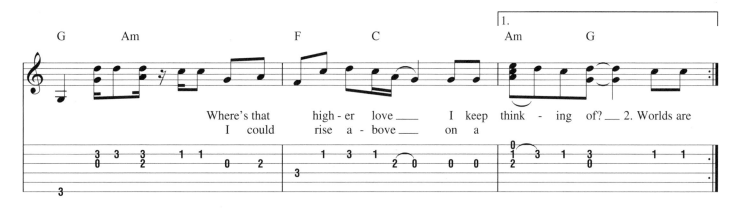

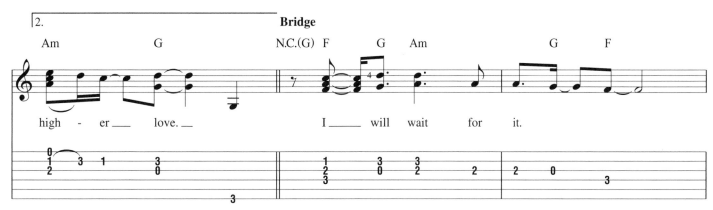

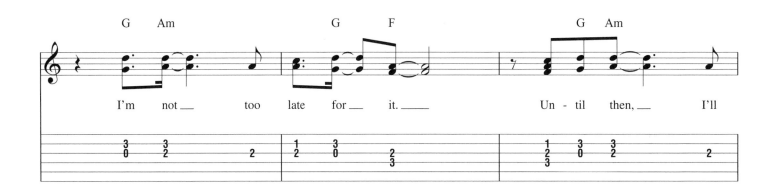
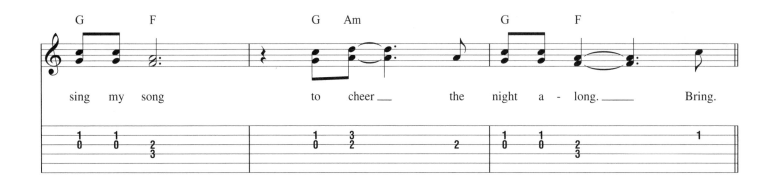

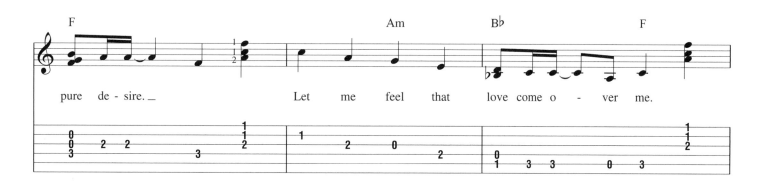

pure de - sire. __   Let me feel that love come o - ver me.

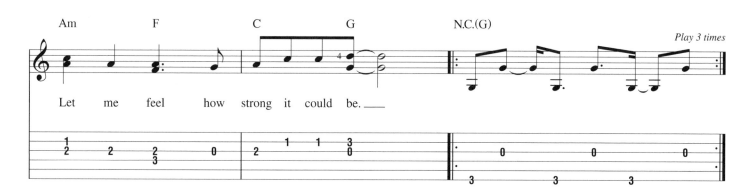

Let me feel how strong it could be. ___

Chorus
w/ Lead Voc. ad lib.

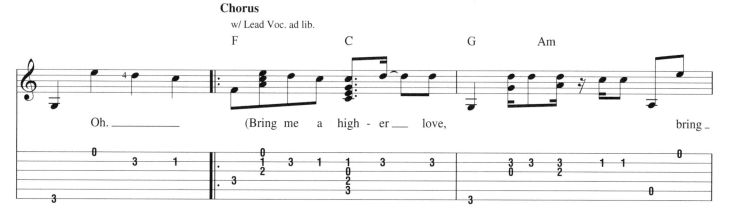

Oh. _____   (Bring me a high - er __ love,   bring _

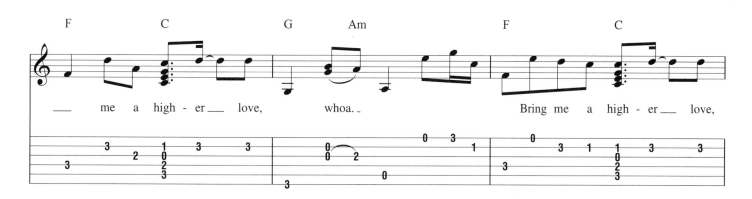

__ me a high - er __ love,   whoa. _   Bring me a high - er __ love,

Repeat and fade

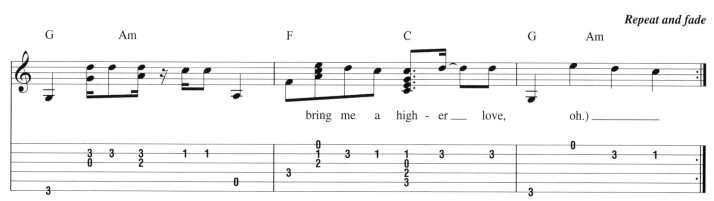

bring me a high - er __ love,   oh.) _____

I Honestly Love You

Words and Music by Jeff Barry and Peter Allen

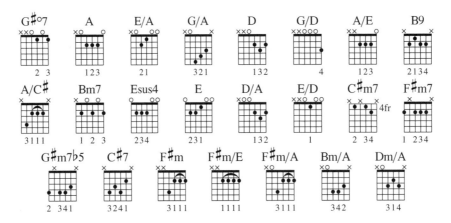

*Capo I

Strum Pattern: 4
Pick Pattern: 5

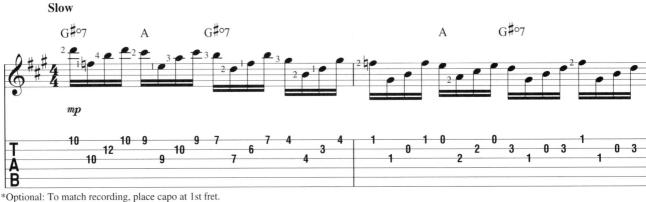

*Optional: To match recording, place capo at 1st fret.

1. May-be I hang a - round here a
2. You don't have to an - swer; I
3. If we both were born in an -

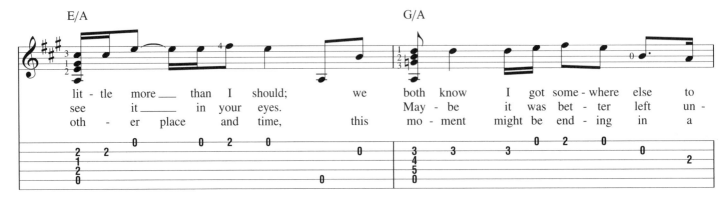

lit - tle more than I should; we both know I got some - where else to
see it in your eyes. May - be it was bet - ter left un -
oth - er place and time, this mo - ment might be end - ing in a

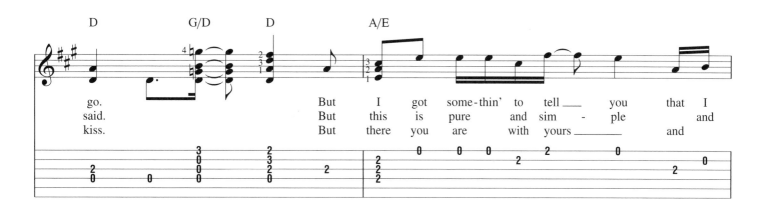

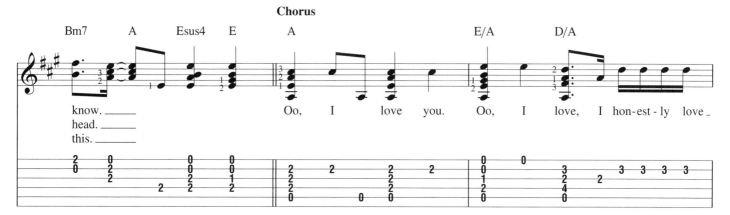

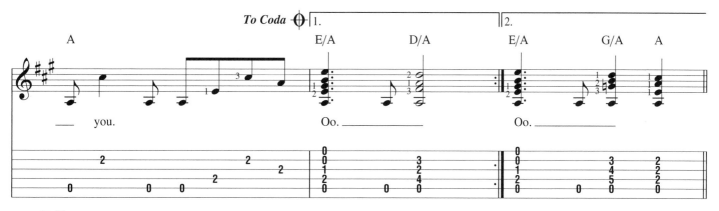

*Sung one octave higher.

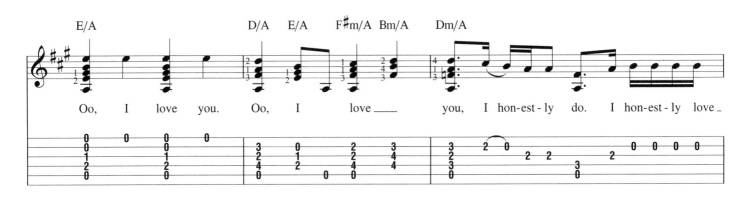

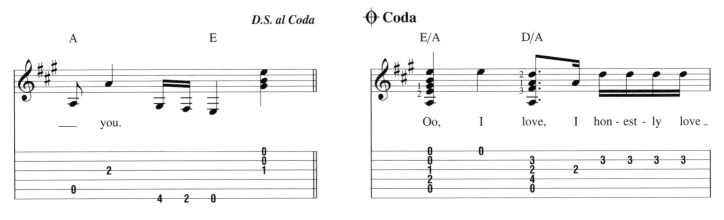

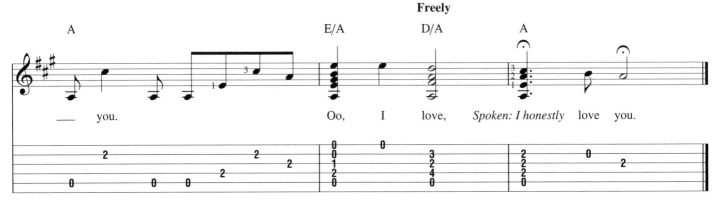

I Left My Heart in San Francisco

Words by Douglas Cross
Music by George Cory

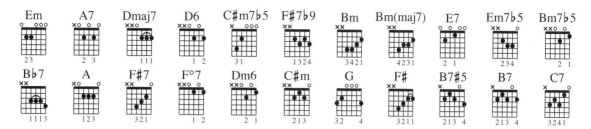

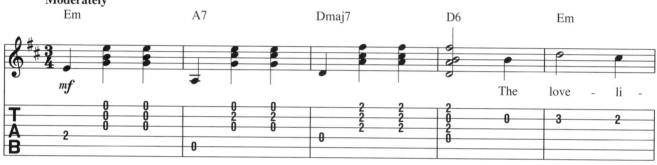

Strum Pattern: 8
Pick Pattern: 8

Intro
Moderately

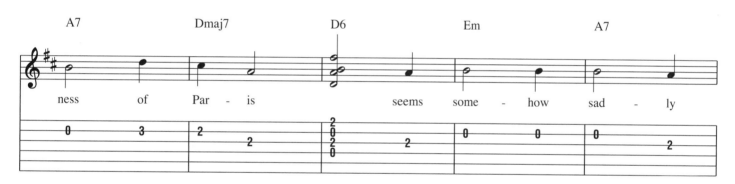

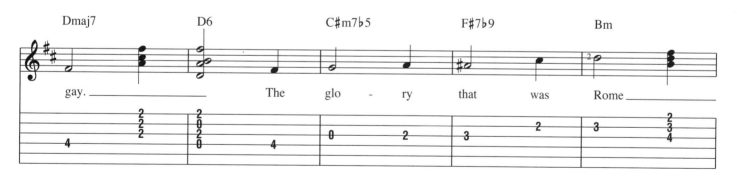

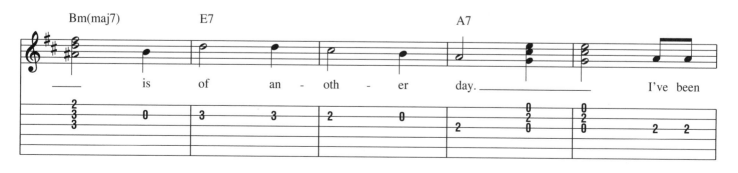

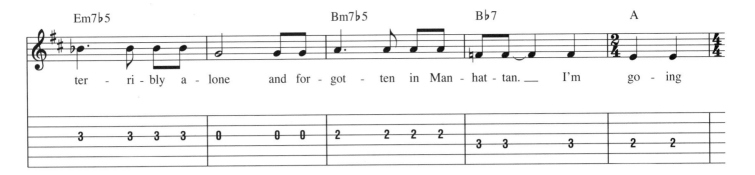

Strum Pattern: 3
Pick Pattern: 3

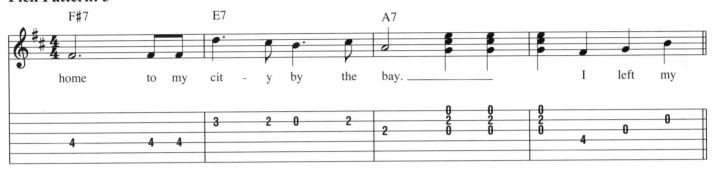

Chorus

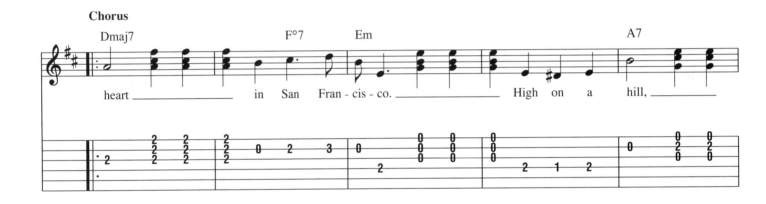

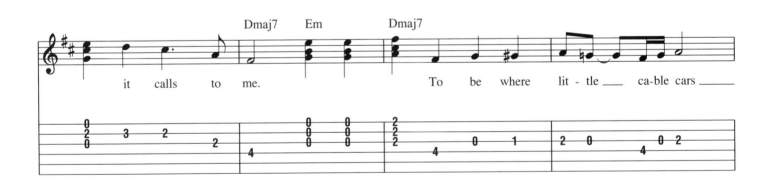

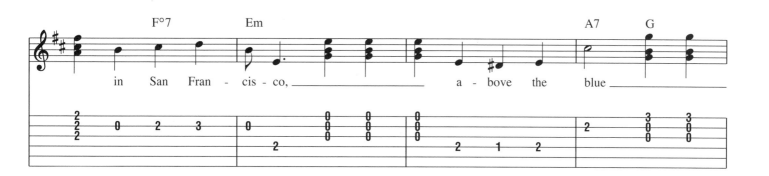

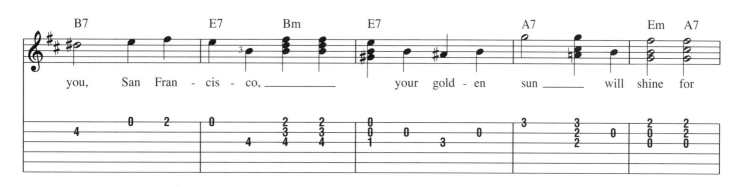

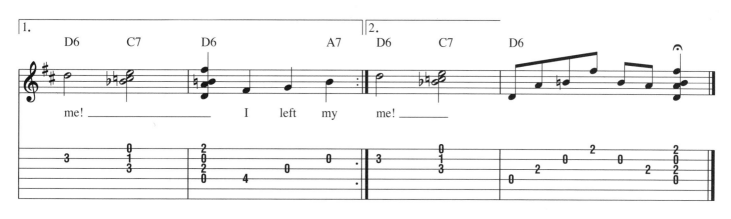

I Will Always Love You

Words and Music by Dolly Parton

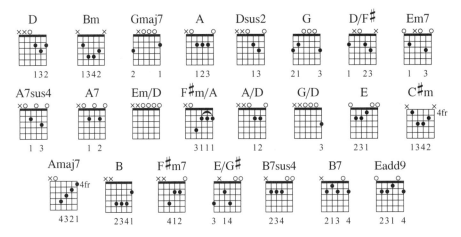

Strum Pattern: 3, 4
Pick Pattern: 4, 5

Verse
Freely

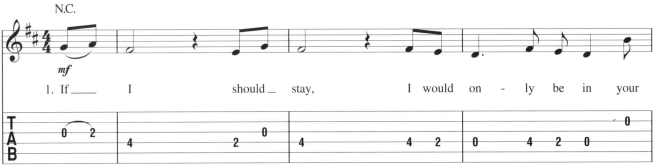

1. If ___ I should ___ stay, I would on - ly be in your

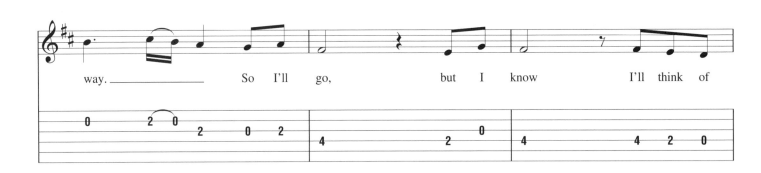

way. ___ So I'll go, but I know I'll think of

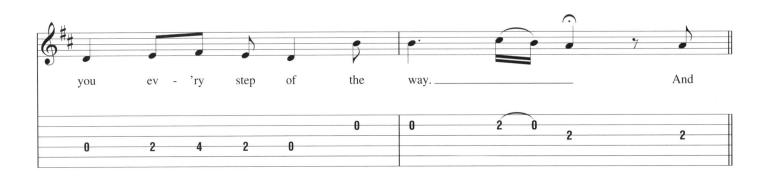

you ev - 'ry step of the way. ___ And

Chorus
Slowly

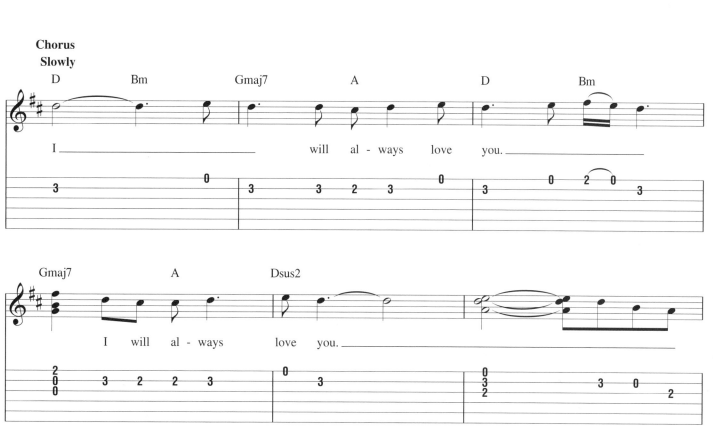

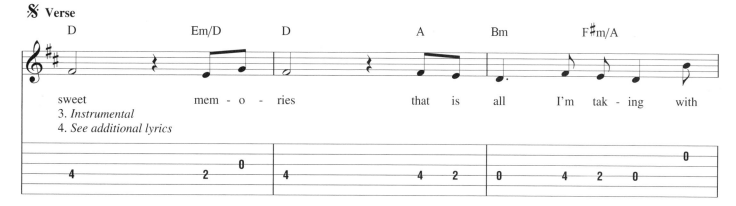

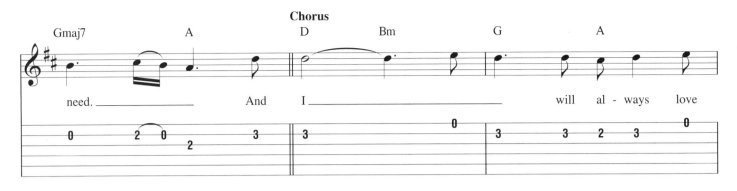

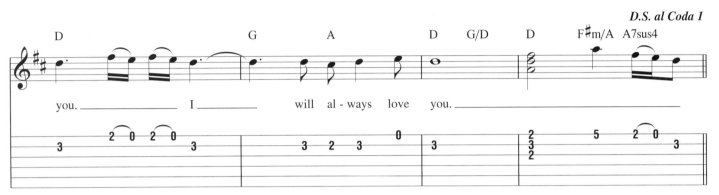

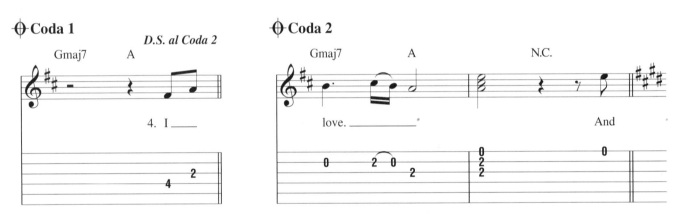

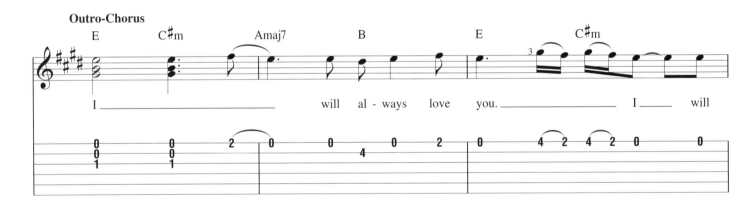

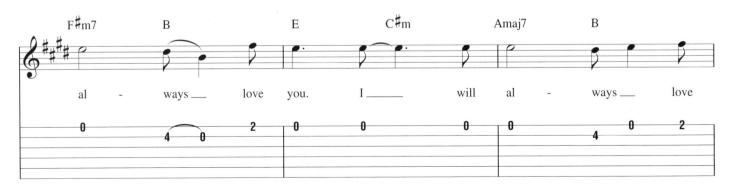

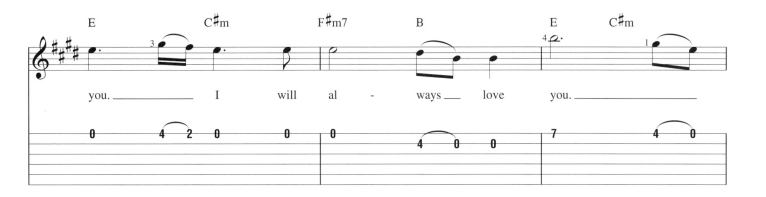

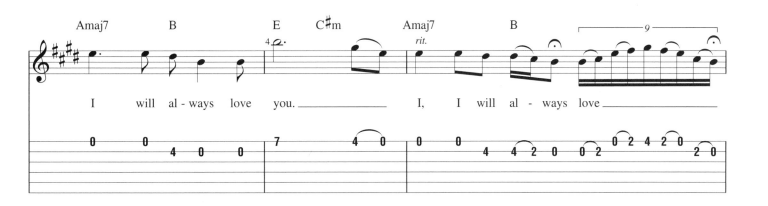

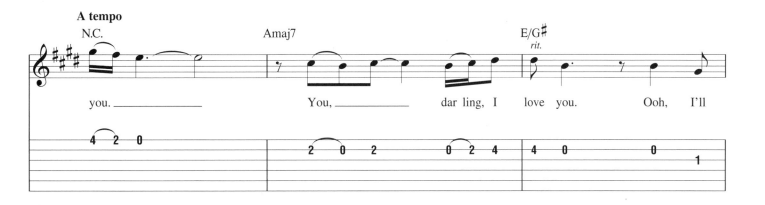

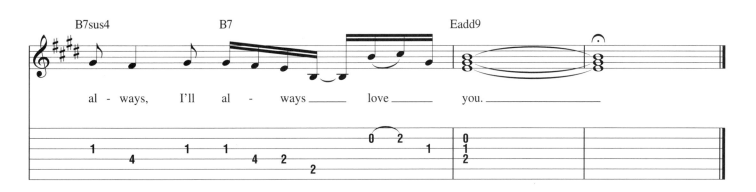

Additional Lyrics

4. I hope life treats you kind.
   And I hope you have all you've dreamed of.
   And I wish to you, joy and happiness.
   But above all this, I wish you love.

It's Too Late

Words and Music by Carole King and Toni Stern

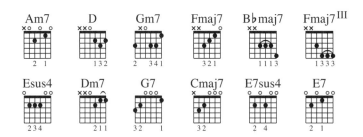

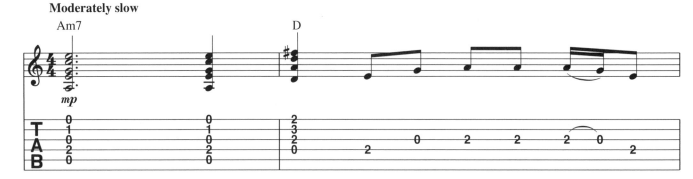

Strum Pattern: 3,4
Pick Pattern: 5,6

Intro

Moderately slow

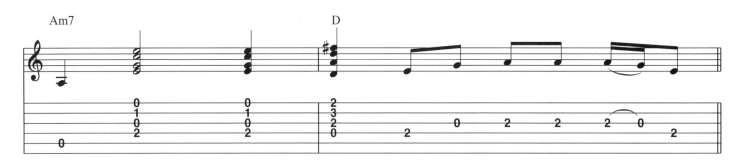

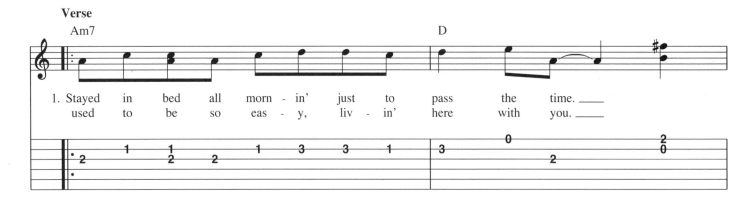

Verse

1. Stayed in bed all mornin' just to pass the time. ____
   used to be so eas - y, liv - in' here with you. ____

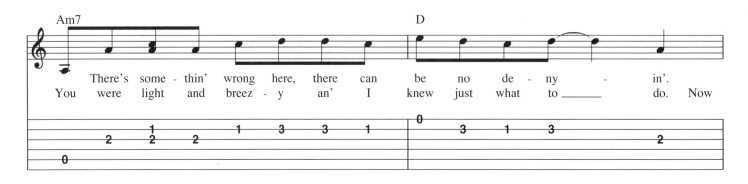

There's some-thin' wrong here, there can be no de-ny - in'.
You were light and breez - y an' I knew just what to ____ do. Now

One of us is chang-in' or may-be we've just stopped try - in'.
you look so un-hap-py and I feel ___ like a fool. _____

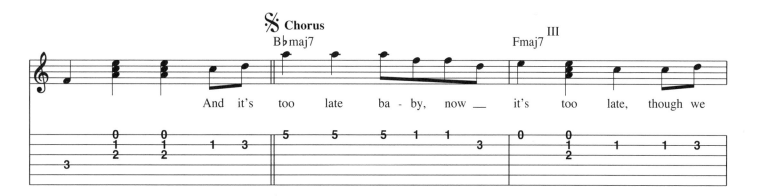

𝄋 **Chorus**

And it's too late ba - by, now ___ it's too late, though we

real - ly did try to make it. Some-thin' in - side has

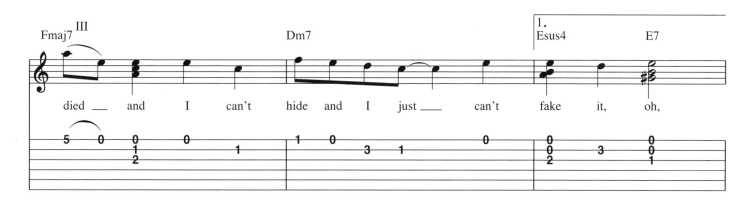

died ___ and I can't hide and I just ___ can't fake it, oh,

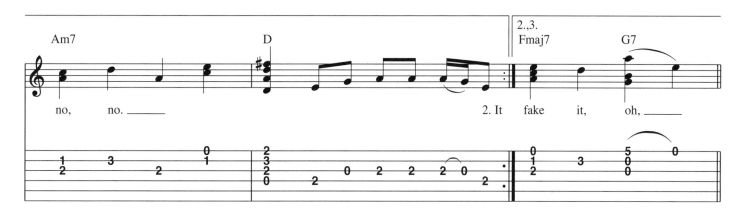

no, no. _____   2. It fake it, oh, _____

Bridge

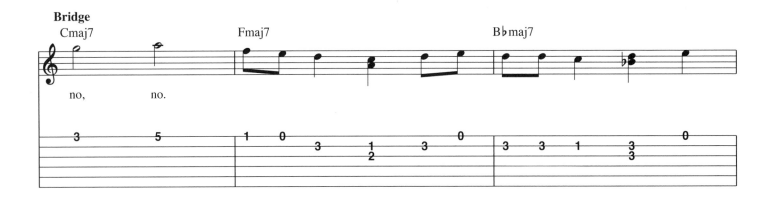

no,   no.

To Coda ⊕

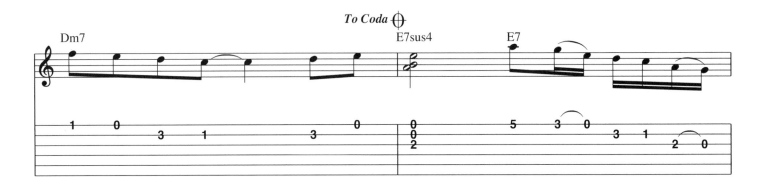

Verse

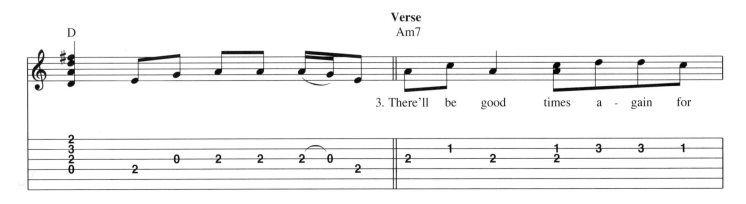

3. There'll be good times a - gain for

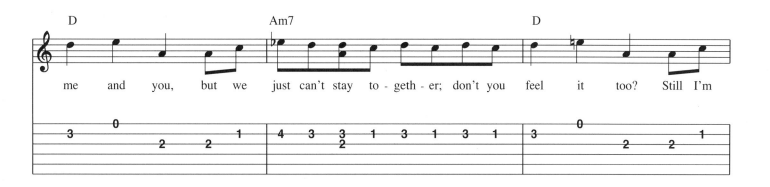

me and you, but we just can't stay to - geth - er; don't you feel it too? Still I'm

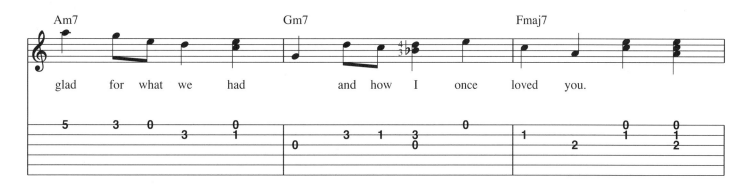

glad for what we had and how I once loved you.

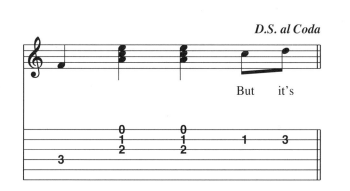

D.S. al Coda

But it's

Coda

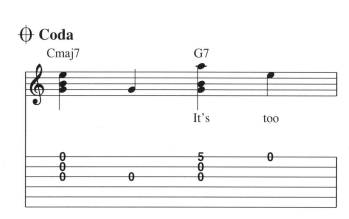

It's too

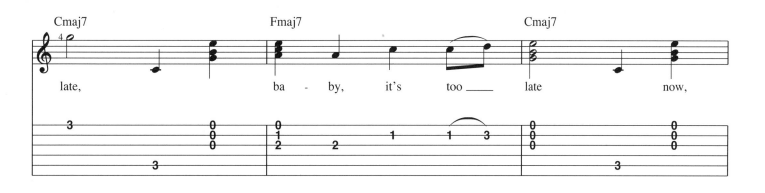

late, ba - by, it's too ___ late now,

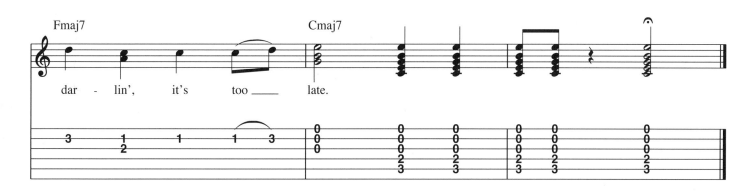

dar - lin', it's too ___ late.

Just the Way You Are

Words and Music by Billy Joel

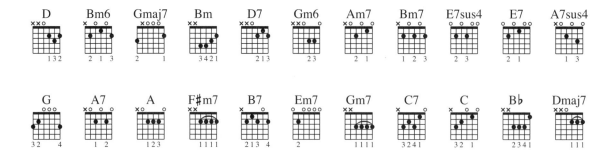

Strum Pattern: 1
Pick Pattern: 2

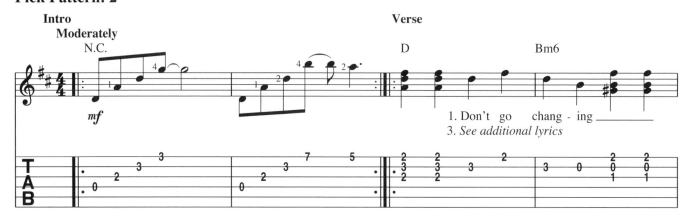

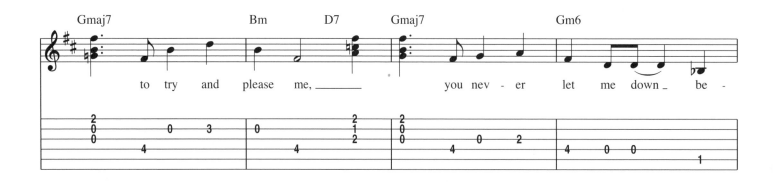

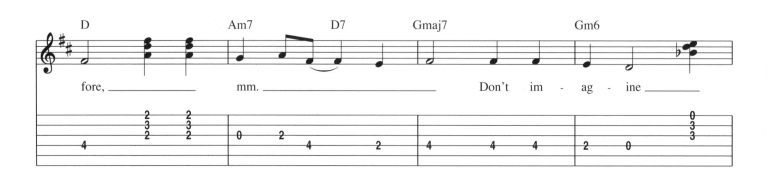

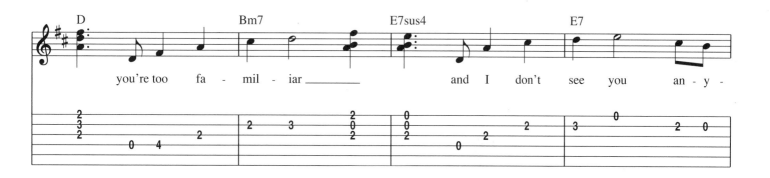

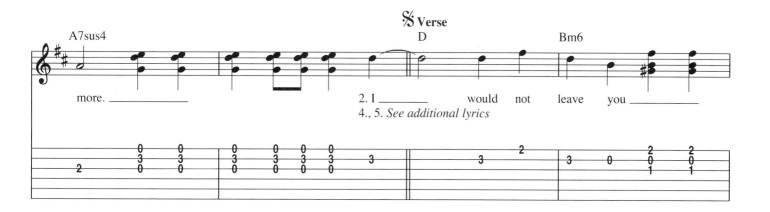

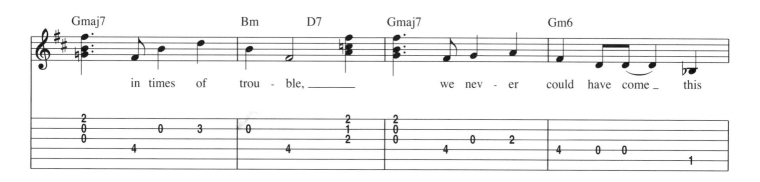

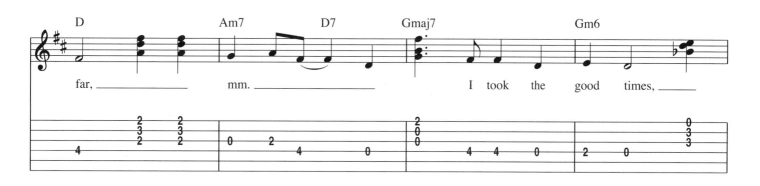

are.

Bridge

I need to know that you will al - ways be _____

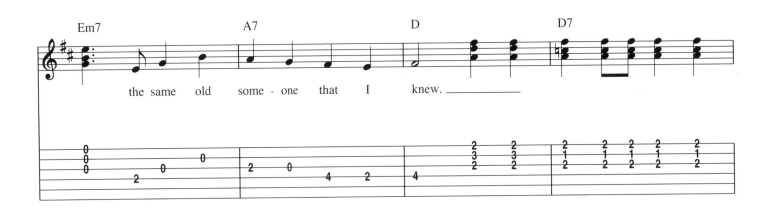

the same old some-one that I knew. _____

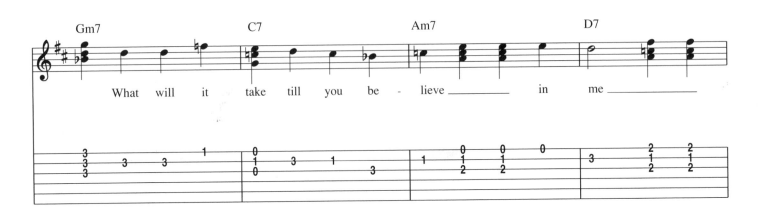

What will it take till you be - lieve _____ in me _____

the way that I be - lieve in you? _____ 5. I ___

✟ Coda

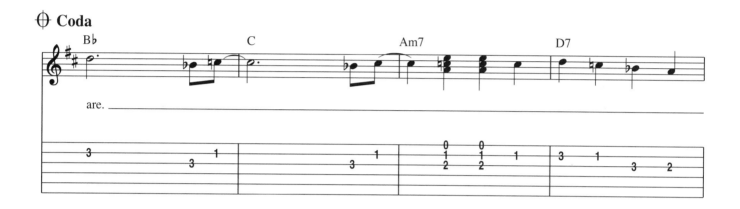

are. _____

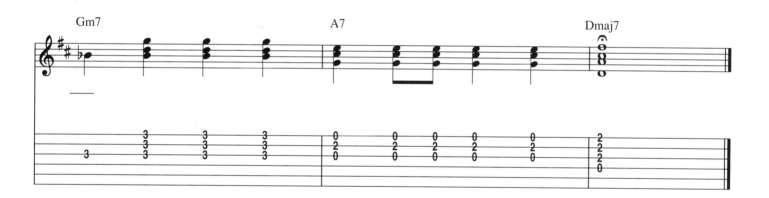

Additional Lyrics

3. Don't go trying some new fashion,
Don't change the color of your hair, mm.
You always have my unspoken passion,
Although I might not seem to care.

4. I don't want clever conversation,
I never want to work that hard, mm.
I just want someone that I can talk to;
I want you just the way you are.

5. I said I love you and that's forever,
And this I promise from the heart, mm.
I could not love you any better,
I love you just the way you are.

Killing Me Softly with His Song

Words by Norman Gimbel
Music by Charles Fox

this young _ boy, a stran - ger to _____ my eyes. _____
would fin - ish, but he just kept _____ right on. _____
this stran - ger, sing - ing clear _____ and strong. _____

𝄋 Chorus

Strum-min' my pain _ with his fin - gers, sing-in' my life _ with his words. _

Kill-ing me soft - ly with his _____ song, kill-ing me soft - ly with his _____ song, tell-in' my whole _

_ life with his _____ words, kill - ing me _____ soft - ly _____ with his

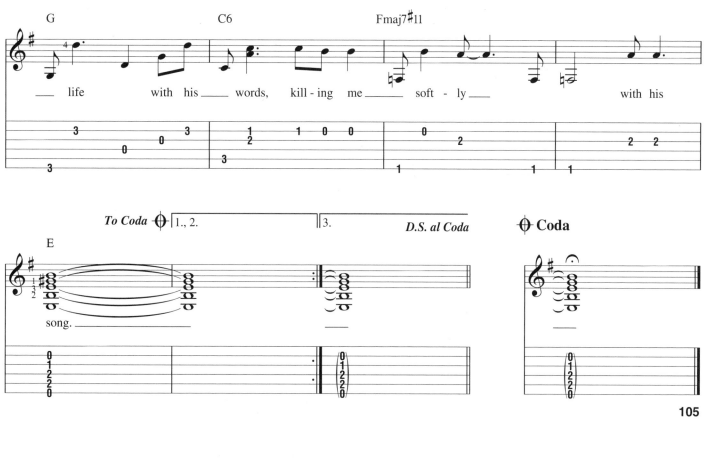

To Coda ⊕ | 1., 2. | 3. | **D.S. al Coda**   **⊕ Coda**

song. _____

Kiss from a Rose

Words and Music by Seal

pill. __ But did you know that when it snows, my eyes be come large and the light that you

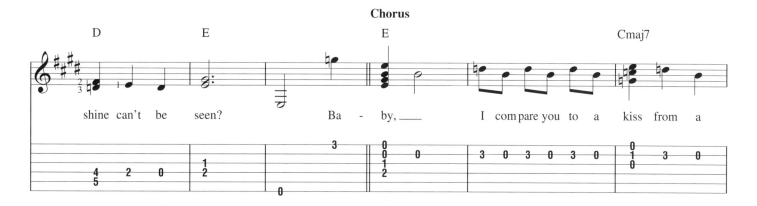

Chorus

shine can't be seen? Ba - by, ___ I com pare you to a kiss from a

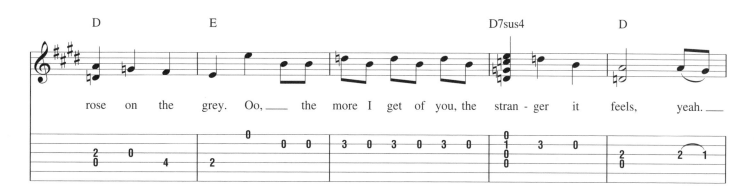

rose on the grey. Oo, ___ the more I get of you, the stran - ger it feels, yeah. ___

3rd time, To Coda 2 ⊕

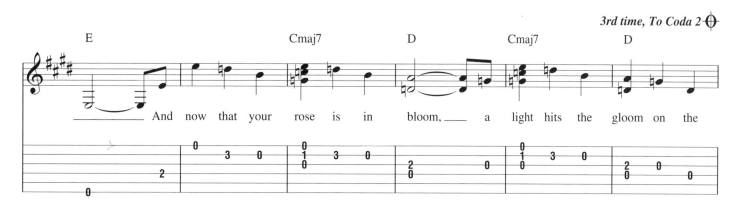

___ And now that your rose is in bloom, ___ a light hits the gloom on the

Interlude

grey. ___ Ba, ya, ya, ba, da, ba, da, da, da, ba, ya, ya. Ba, ya,
Instrumental

ya, ba, da, ba, da, da, da, ba, ya, ya. 2. There ___ is so much a man can

tell you, so much he can say. ___ You ___ re-main my pow-er, my

pleas-ure, my pain. Ba - by, ___ to me you're like a grow'n'ad-

D.S. al Coda 1

dic-tion that I can't de - ny. Won't you tell me, is that health-y, babe? But did you

Coda 1

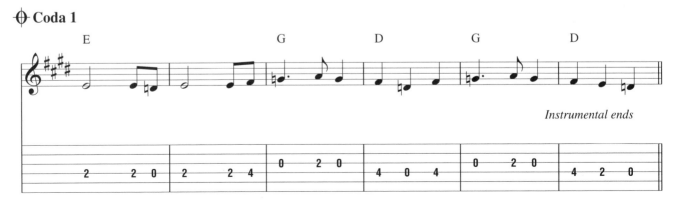

Instrumental ends

108

Bridge

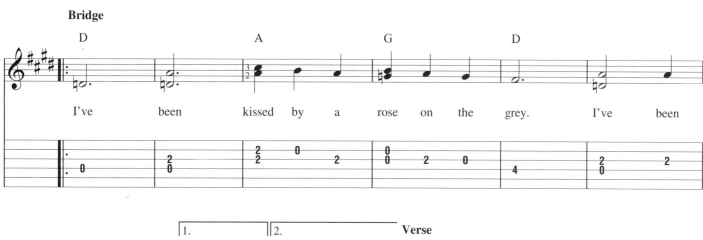

I've been kissed by a rose on the grey. I've been

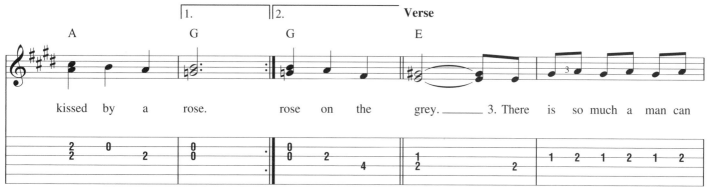

1. | 2. | **Verse**

kissed by a rose. rose on the grey. ___ 3. There is so much a man can

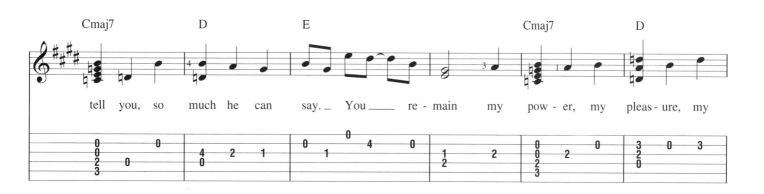

tell you, so much he can say. _ You ___ re - main my pow - er, my pleas - ure, my

pain. To me you're like a grow'n' ad - dic - tion that I can't de -

D.S. al Coda 2

ny. ___ Now, won't you tell me, is that health - y, ba - by? But did you

Coda 2

grey. ___ Yes, I com-pare you to a kiss from a rose on the grey. Oo, ___ the

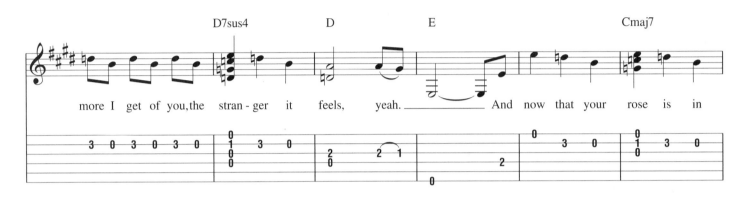

more I get of you, the stran-ger it feels, yeah. ___ And now that your rose is in

Outro

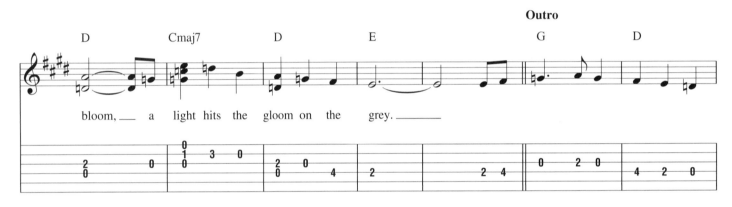

bloom, ___ a light hits the gloom on the grey. ___

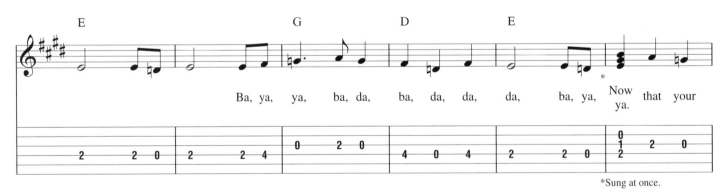

Ba, ya, ya, ba, da, ba, da, da, da, ba, ya, Now that your
ya.

Sung at once.

Freely

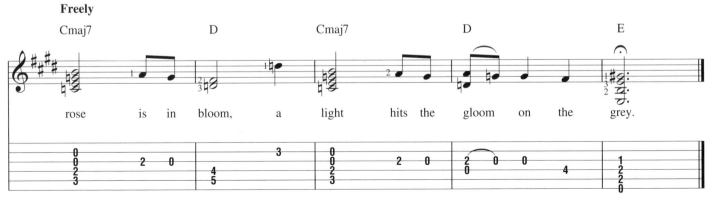

rose is in bloom, a light hits the gloom on the grey.

Love Will Keep Us Together

Words and Music by Neil Sedaka and Howard Greenfield

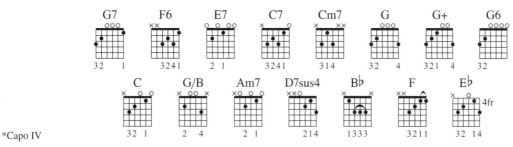

*Capo IV

Strum Pattern: 4
Pick Pattern: 4

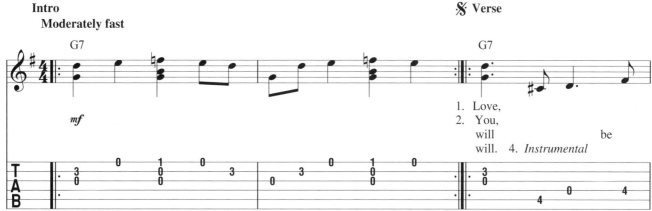

*Optional: To match recording, place capo at 4th fret.

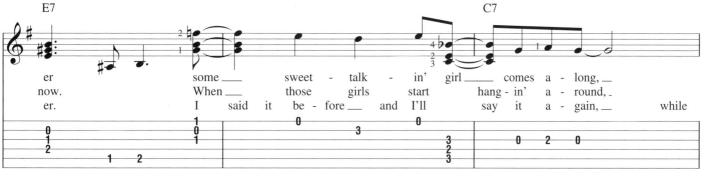

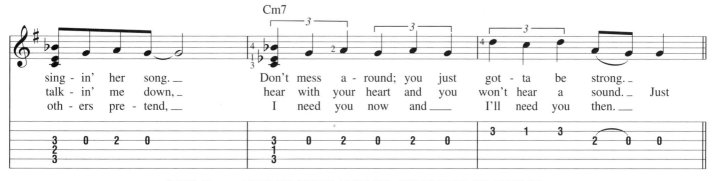

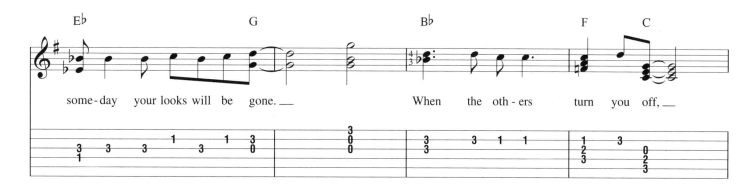

some-day your looks will be gone. ___ When the oth-ers turn you off, ___

D.S. al Coda 1
(take 2nd ending)

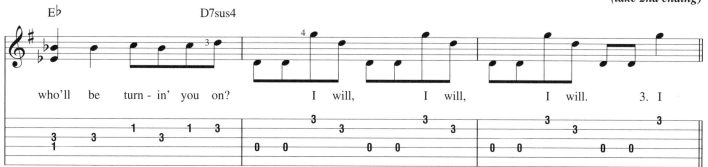

who'll be turn-in' you on? I will, I will, I will. 3. I

⊕ Coda 1

D.S. al Coda 2

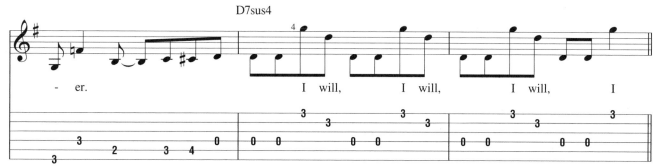

-er. I will, I will, I will, I

⊕ Coda 2

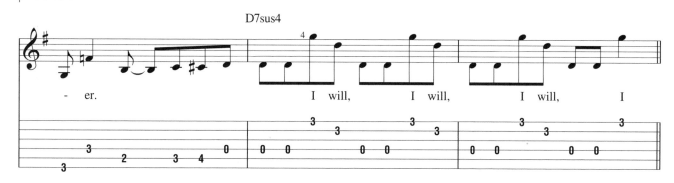

-er. I will, I will, I will, I

Outro

Repeat and fade

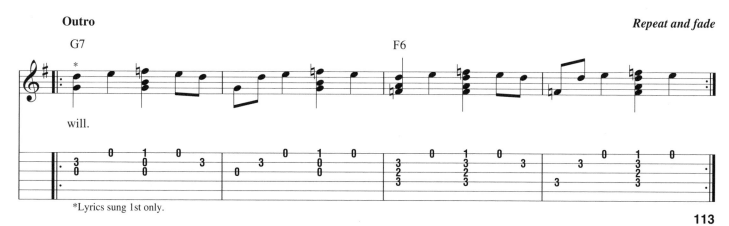

will.

*Lyrics sung 1st only.

Mack the Knife

from THE THREEPENNY OPERA

English Words by Marc Blitzstein
Original German Words by Bert Brecht
Music by Kurt Weill

*Optional: To match recording, place capo at 3rd fret.

Additional Lyrics

4. A, there's a tugboat down by the river, don't ya know,
   Where a cement bag's just a droopin' on down.
   Whoa, that cement is just, it's there for the weight, dear,
   Five'll get ya ten ol' Mackie's back in town.

5. Now'd you hear 'bout Louie Miller? He disappeared, babe,
   After drawin' out all his hard-earned cash.
   And now Mackheath spends just like a sailor.
   Could it be our boy's done somethin' rash?

6. Now, Jenny Diver, yeah, Sukey Tawdry,
   Oo, Miss Lotte Lenya, and Lucy Brown;
   Oh, the line forms on the right, babe,
   Now that Mackie's back in town.

7. Ah, said Jenny Diver, whoa, Sukey Tawdry,
   Look out a Miss Lotte Lenya and ol' Lucy Brown;
   Yes, that line forms on the right, babe,
   Now that Mackie's back in town.
   Spoken: Look out, ol' Mackie is back!

Moon River

from the Paramount Picture BREAKFAST AT TIFFANY'S

Words by Johnny Mercer
Music by Henry Mancini

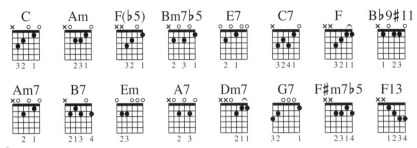

Strum Pattern: 8
Pick Pattern: 8

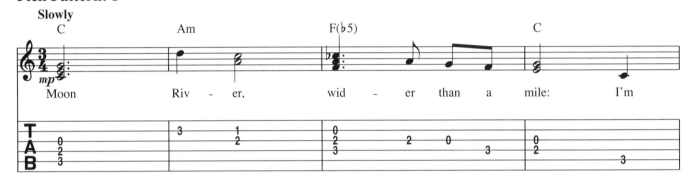

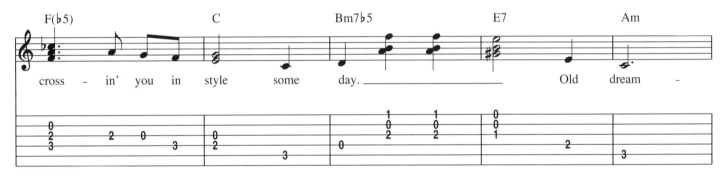

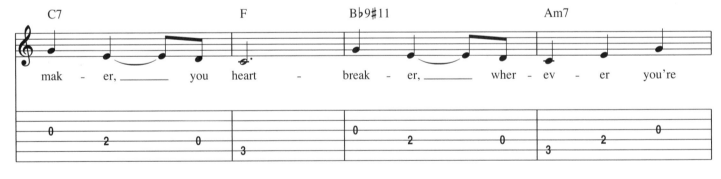

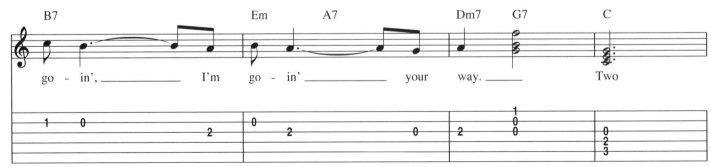

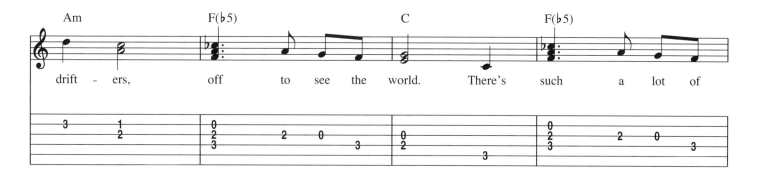

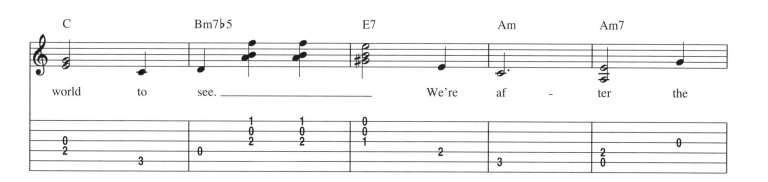

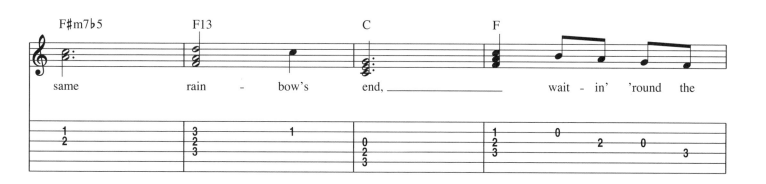

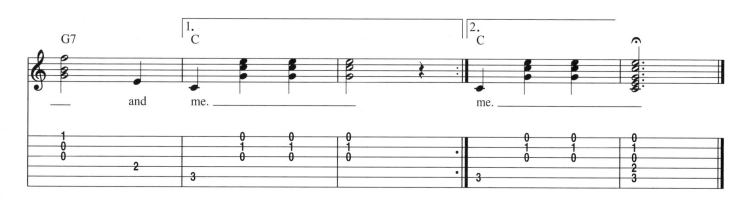

Mrs. Robinson

from THE GRADUATE

Words and Music by Paul Simon

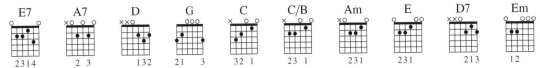

E7 A7 D G C C/B Am E D7 Em

*Capo II

Strum Pattern: 3, 5
Pick Pattern: 1, 3

Intro
Moderately fast

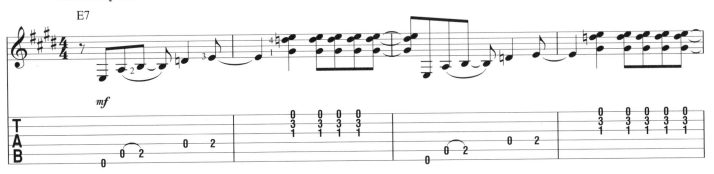

*Optional: To match recording, place capo at 2nd fret.

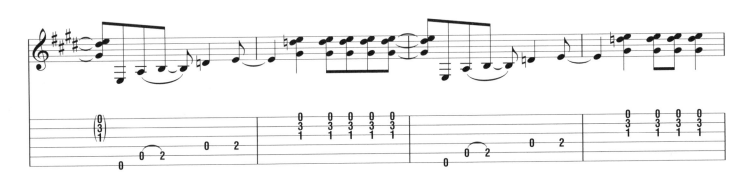

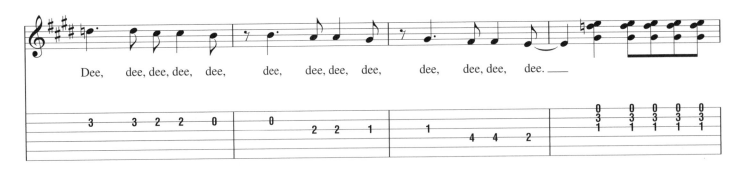

Dee, dee, dee, dee, dee, dee, dee, dee, dee, dee, dee, dee, dee. ___

Doo, doo, doo, doo, doo, doo, doo, doo, doo. ___

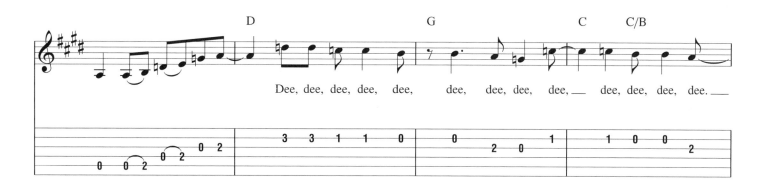

Dee, dee, dee, dee, dee, dee, dee, dee, dee, ___ dee, dee, dee, dee. ___

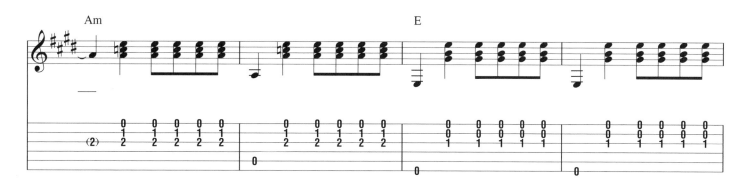

𝄋 Chorus

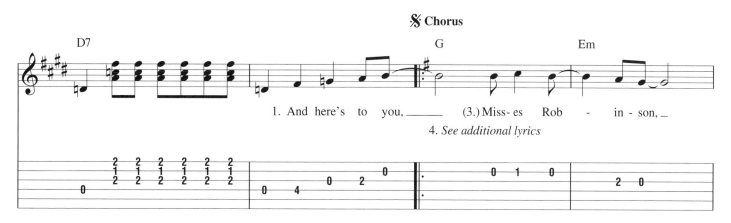

1. And here's to you, ___ (3.) Miss- es Rob - in - son, ___
4. *See additional lyrics*

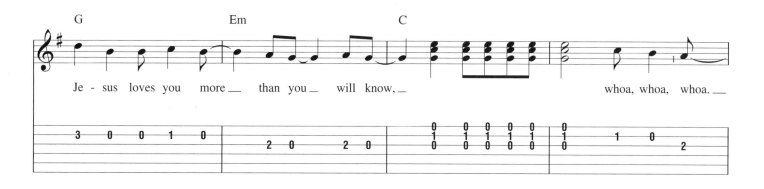

Je - sus loves you more ___ than you ___ will know, ___ whoa, whoa, whoa. ___

God bless you please, ___ Miss- es Ro - bin - son. ___

119

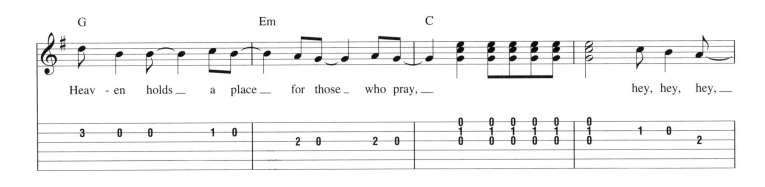

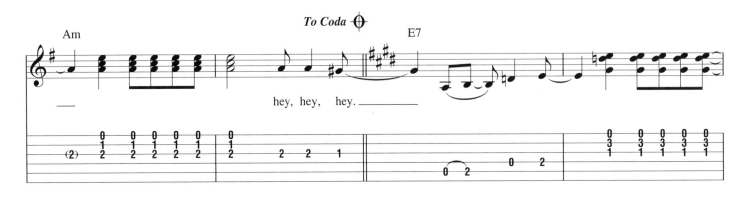

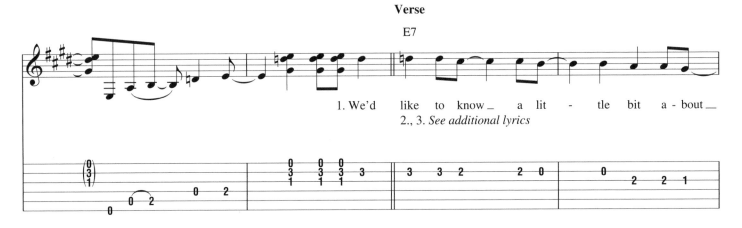

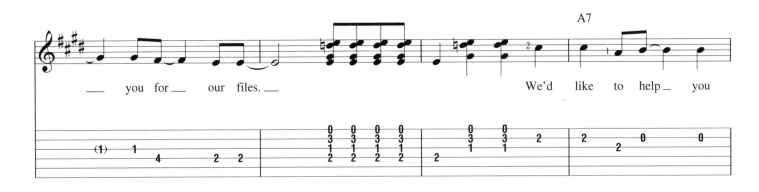

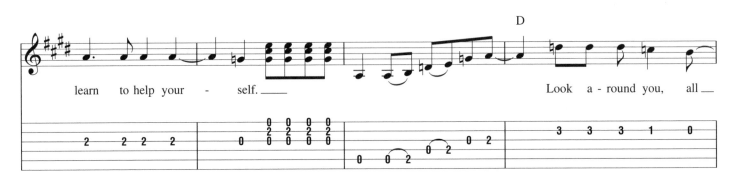

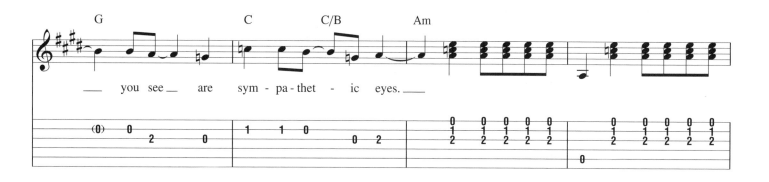

you see — are sym-pa-thet-ic eyes. —

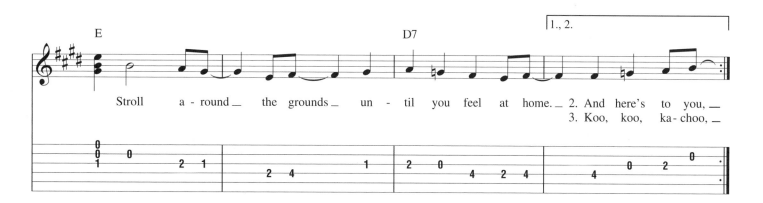

Stroll a-round — the grounds — un-til you feel at home. — 2. And here's to you, —

3. Koo, koo, ka-choo, —

3.

D.S. al Coda

— 4. Where have you gone, —

⊕ **Coda**

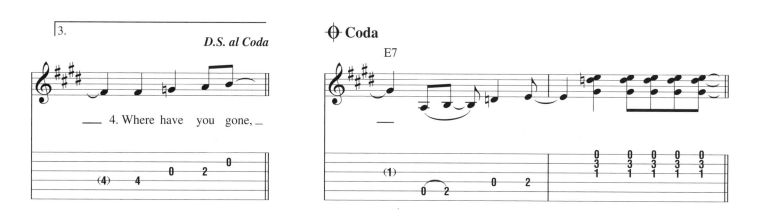

Outro

Repeat and fade

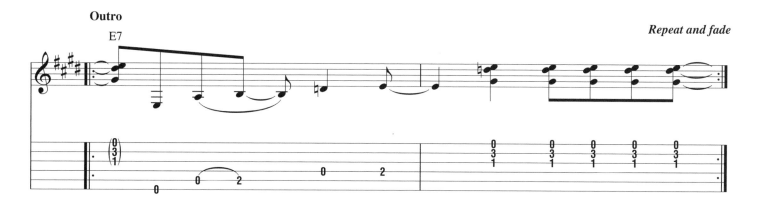

Additional Lyrics

2. Hide it in a hiding place where no one ever goes.
Put in in your pantry with your cupcakes.
It's a little secret, just the Robinsons' affair.
Most of all you've got to hide it from the kids.

3. Sitting on a sofa on a Sunday afternoon.
Going to the candidates debate.
Laugh about it, shout about it when you've got to choose.
Ev'ry way you look at this you lose.

Chorus 4. Where have you gone, Joe DiMaggio?
A nation turns its lonely eyes to you, woo, woo, woo.
What's that you say, Mrs. Robinson?
Joltin' Joe has left and gone away,
Hey, hey, hey, hey, hey, hey.

My Heart Will Go On
(Love Theme from 'Titanic')
from the Paramount and Twentieth Century Fox Motion Picture TITANIC

Music by James Horner
Lyric by Will Jennings

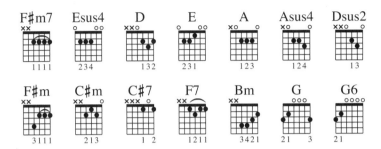

Strum Pattern: 3
Pick Pattern: 3

Intro
Moderately

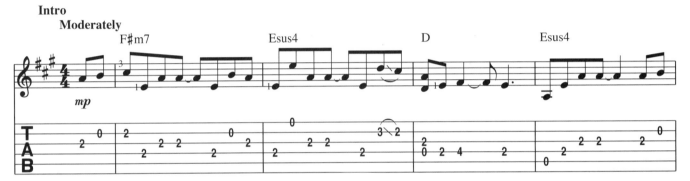

Verse

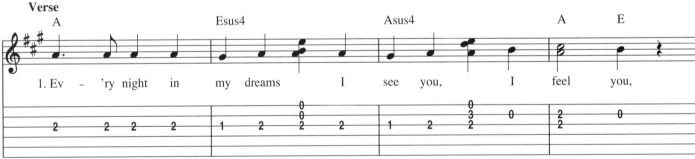

1. Ev - 'ry night in my dreams I see you, I feel you,

that is how I know you go on. _____

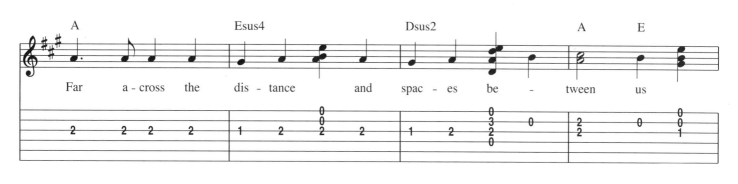

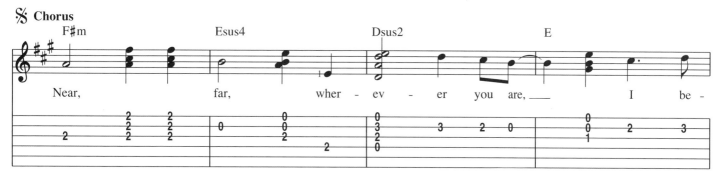

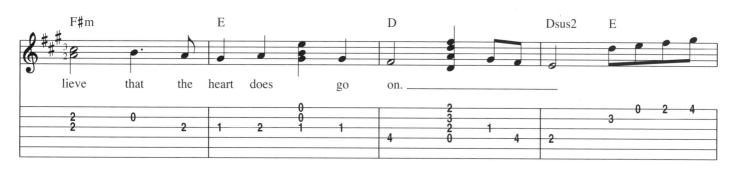

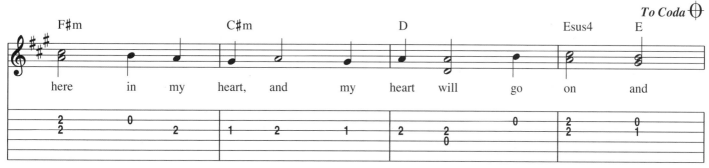

Need You Now

Words and Music by Hillary Scott, Charles Kelley, Dave Haywood and Josh Kear

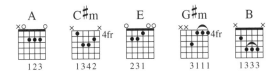

Strum Pattern: 1, 2
Pick Pattern: 2, 4

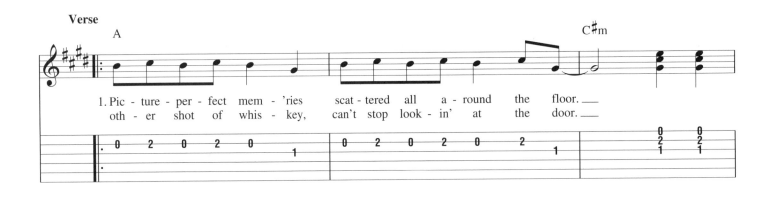

1. Pic - ture - per - fect mem - 'ries, scat - tered all a - round the floor. ___
oth - er shot of whis - key, can't stop look - in' at the door. ___

Reach - in' for the phone 'cause I can't fight it an - y - more. ___
Wish - in' you'd come sweep - in' in the way you did be - fore. ___

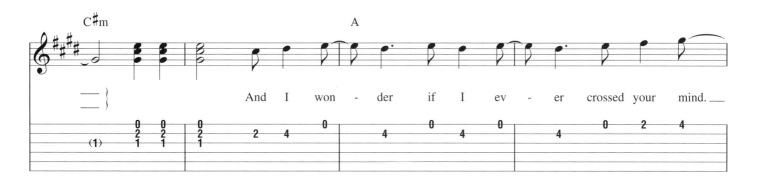

And I won - der if I ev - er crossed your mind. —

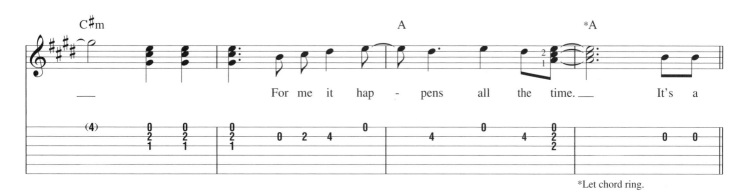

— For me it hap - pens all the time. — It's a

*Let chord ring.

𝄋 Chorus

quar - ter af - ter one. {1., 3. I'm ___ all a - lone,} and I need ___ you now. —
{2. I'm ___ a lit - tle drunk,}

**4th position

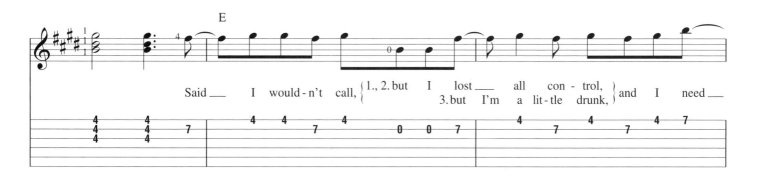

Said ___ I would - n't call, {1., 2. but I lost ___ all con - trol,} and I need ___
{3. but I'm a lit - tle drunk,}

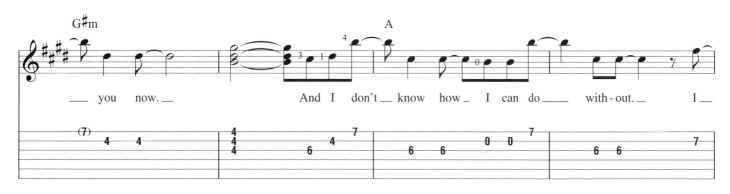

___ you now. ___ And I don't ___ know how ___ I can do ___ with - out. ___ I ___

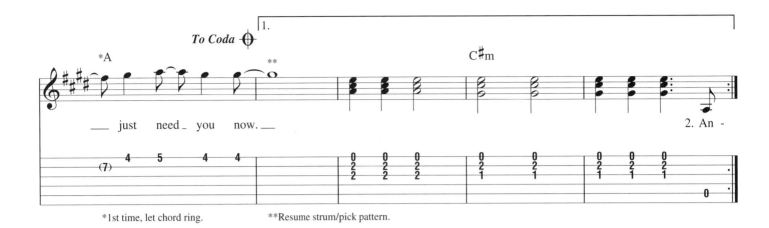

*1st time, let chord ring. **Resume strum/pick pattern.

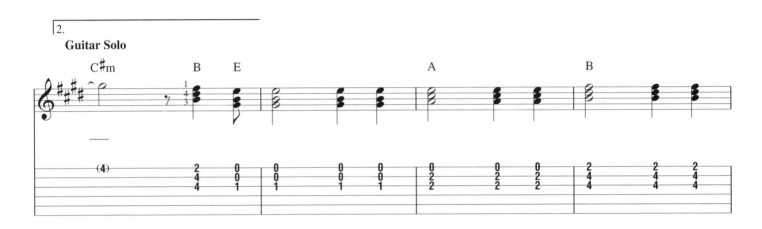

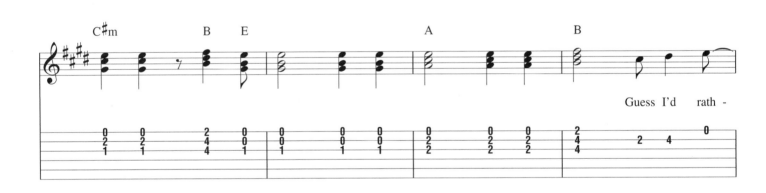

***Let chords ring, next 4 meas.

⊕ Coda

Outro

I _____ just need __ you now. __

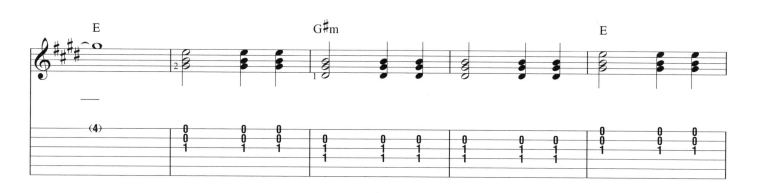

Oh, __ ba - by, I need __ you now. __

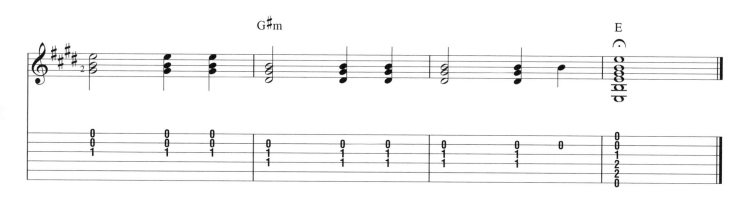

Not Ready to Make Nice

Words and Music by Dan Wilson, Emily Robison, Martie Maguire and Natalie Maines

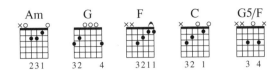

*Capo VI

Strum Pattern: 6
Pick Pattern: 6

Intro
Moderately slow

*Optional: To match recording, place capo at 6th fret.

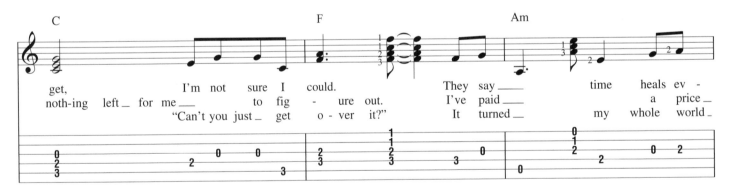

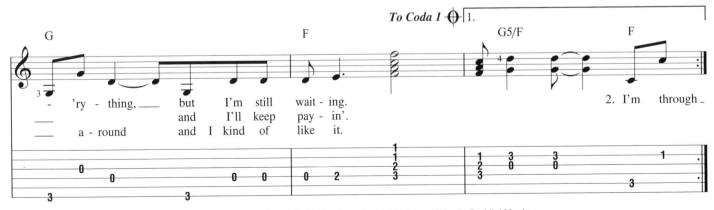

§ § **Chorus**

I'm not read-y to make _ nice, _ I'm not read-y to back _ down. _ I'm still

mad as hell and I don't have time to go round and round _ and round. It's too late to make _ it right. I prob-'ly

To Coda 2 ⊕

would-n't if I could, _ 'cause I'm mad as hell, _ can't bring my-self to do what it is ___ you think I should. _

D.S. al Coda 1   ⊕ **Coda 1**   **Verse**

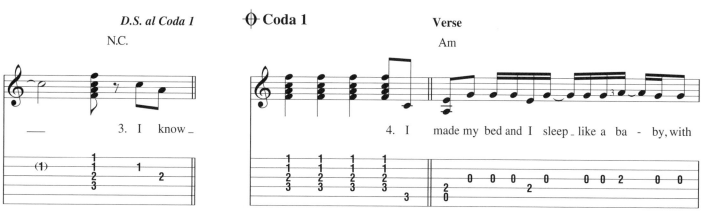

3. I know _   4. I made my bed and I sleep _ like a ba - by, with

no re - grets. And I don't _ mind say-in' it's a sad, sad, sto-ry when a moth-er will teach _ her

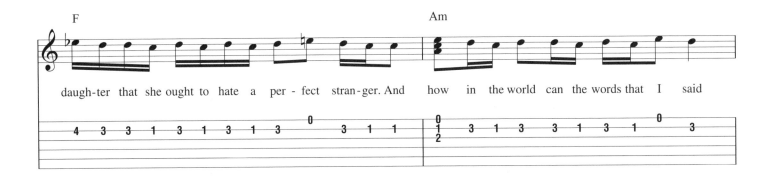

daugh-ter that she ought to hate a per-fect stran-ger. And how in the world can the words that I said

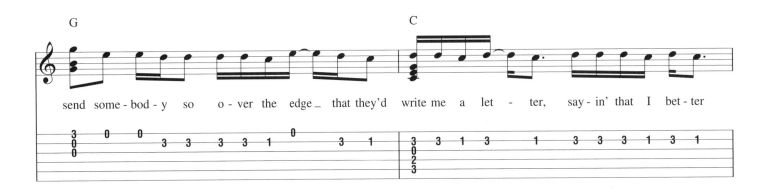

send some-bod-y so o-ver the edge _ that they'd write me a let-ter, say-in' that I bet-ter

Interlude

shut up and sing or my life will be o-ver? _____

D.S.S. al Coda 2

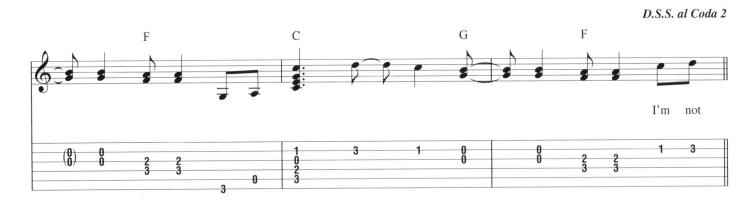

I'm not

✦ **Coda 2**

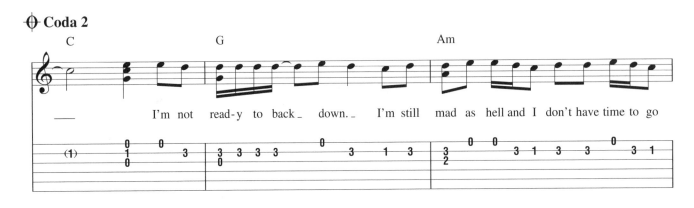

_ I'm not read-y to back _ down. _ I'm still mad as hell and I don't have time to go

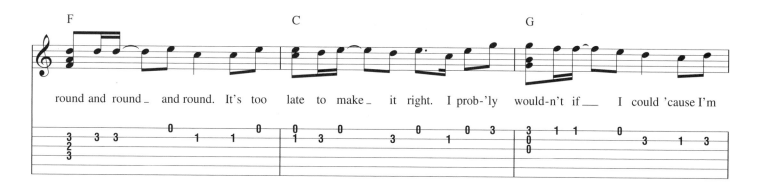

round and round _ and round. It's too late to make _ it right. I prob-'ly would-n't if _ I could 'cause I'm

mad as hell, _ can't bring my-self to do what it is ___ you think I should, _

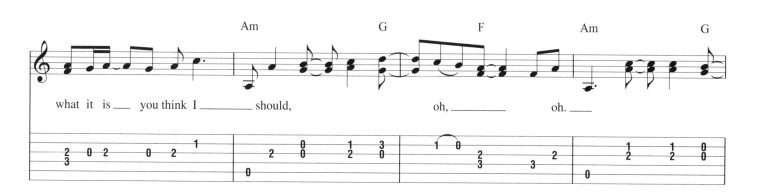

what it is ___ you think I ___ should, oh, ____ oh. ____

Outro-Verse

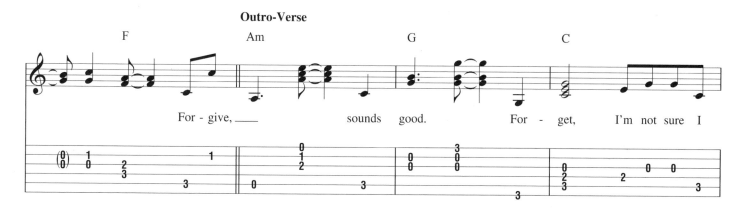

For - give, ____ sounds good. For - get, I'm not sure I

could. They say ____ time heals ev - 'ry - thing, _ but I'm still wait - ing. ____

Please Read the Letter

Words and Music by Robert Plant, Jimmy Page, Michael Pearson and Stephen Jones

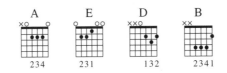

Strum Pattern: 3
Pick Pattern: 3

Intro
Moderately slow

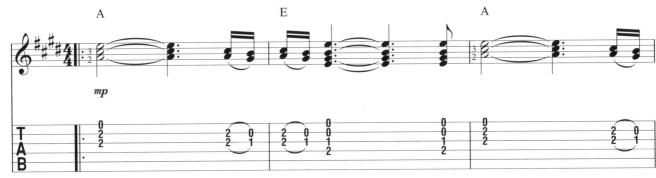

Verse

1. Caught out run - ning _ with just a lit - tle too much to hide. _
2. Too late, too late, a fool could read the signs. _

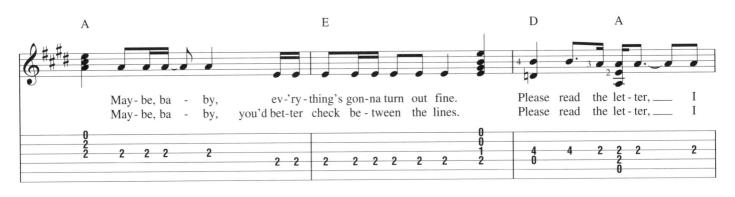

May - be, ba - by, ev - 'ry - thing's gon - na turn out fine.
May - be, ba - by, you'd bet - ter check be - tween the lines.
Please read the let - ter, ___ I
Please read the let - ter, ___ I

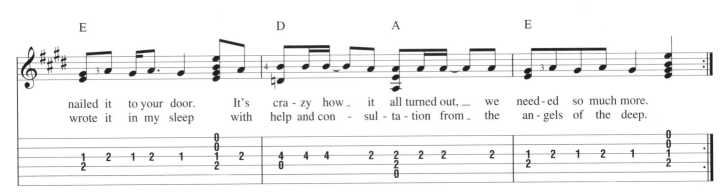

nailed it to your door. It's cra - zy how _ it all turned out, _ we need - ed so much more.
wrote it in my sleep with help and con - sul - ta - tion from _ the an - gels of the deep.

ah, _____ ah, _____ ah. _____

Chorus

Violin Solo

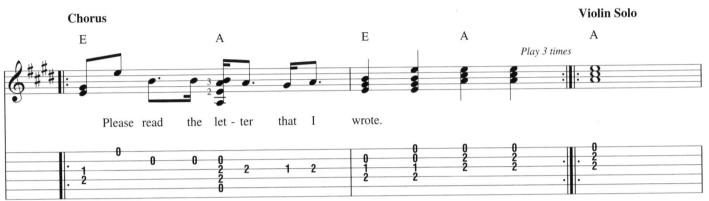

Please read the let-ter that I wrote.

Play 3 times

2nd time, D.S. al Coda

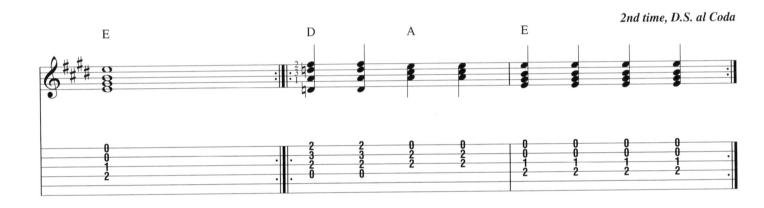

⊕ Coda

Please read the let-ter, ___ I nailed it to your door. It's cra-zy how ___ it all turned out, we

Chorus

Repeat and fade

need-ed so much more. Please read the let-ter that I wrote.
5th time till fade, w/ Voc. & Instrumental ad lib.

Rosanna

Words and Music by David Paich

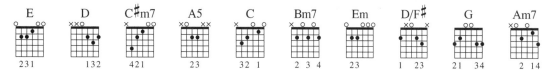

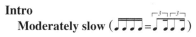

*Capo III

Strum Pattern: 1
Pick Pattern: 5

Intro
Moderately slow

*Optional: To match recording, place capo at 3rd fret.

Verse

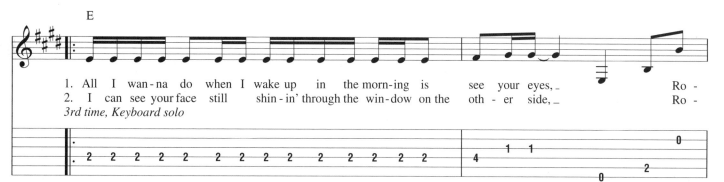

1. All I wan-na do when I wake up in the morn-ing is see your eyes,_ Ro -
2. I can see your face still shin-in' through the win-dow on the oth-er side,_ Ro -
3rd time, Keyboard solo

san - na,_ Ro - san - na._ Nev - er thought that a girl like you could ev - er
san - na,_ Ro - san - na._ I did - n't know that a girl like you could make me

care for me,_ Ro - san - na._
feel so sad,_ Ro - san - na._

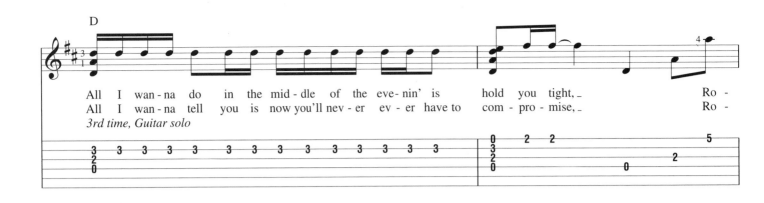

All I wan-na do in the mid-dle of the eve-nin' is hold you tight,___ Ro-
All I wan-na tell you is now you'll nev-er ev-er have to com-pro-mise,___ Ro-

3rd time, Guitar solo

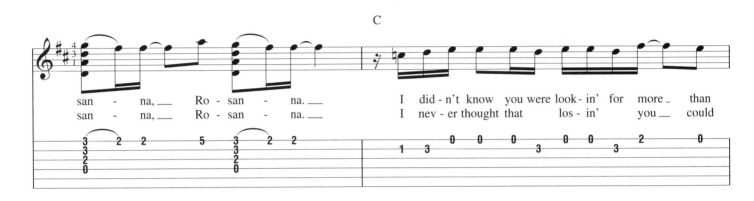

C

san - na,___ Ro-san - na.___ I did-n't know you were look-in' for more___ than
san - na,___ Ro-san - na.___ I nev-er thought that los-in' you___ could

Pre-Chorus

Bm7   Em

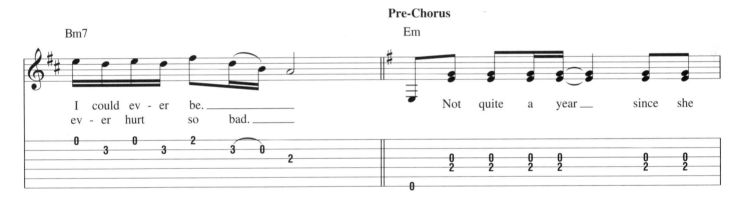

I could ev-er be._____ Not quite a year___ since she
ev-er hurt so bad._____

D/F# G   C   G   D   Em

went a-way,___ Ro-san - na,_____ yeah. _ Now she's gone and I

D/F# G   C   G   D

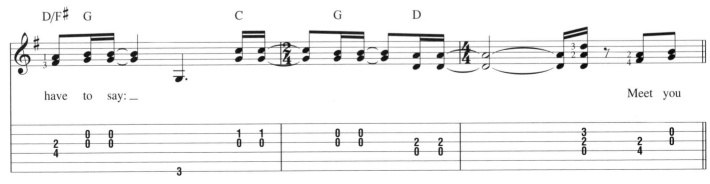

have to say: _   Meet you

Rehab

Words and Music by Amy Winehouse

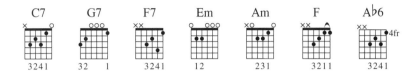

Strum Pattern: 6
Pick Pattern: 4

Chorus
Moderately

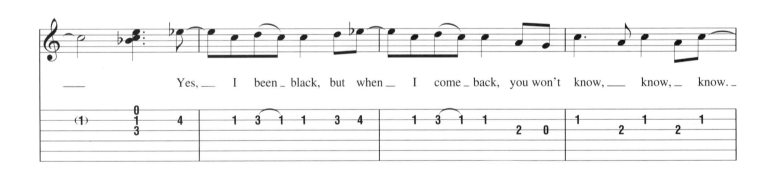

They tried to make me go to re - hab, I ___ said, ___ "No, ___ no, ___ no."

Yes, ___ I been ___ black, but when ___ I come ___ back, you won't know, ___ know, ___ know.

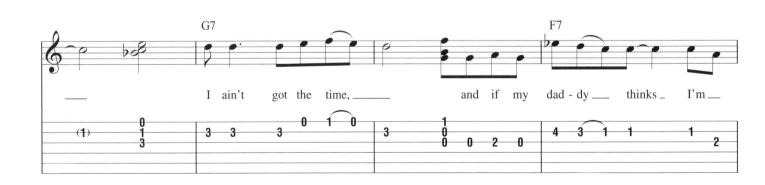

I ain't got the time, ___ and if my dad - dy ___ thinks ___ I'm

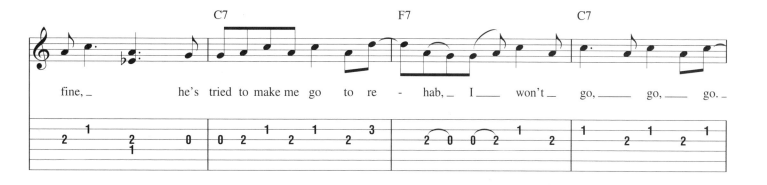

fine, ___ he's tried to make me go to re - hab, I ___ won't ___ go, ___ go, ___ go. _

𝄋 Verse

1. I'd rath - er be ___ at home _____ with Ray.
2., 3. *See additional lyrics*

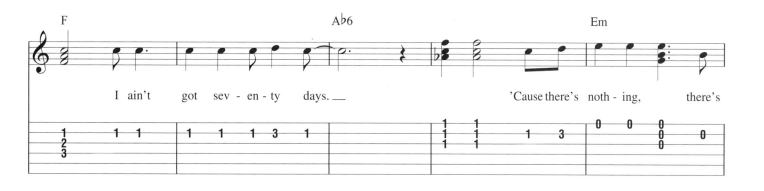

I ain't got sev - en - ty days. ___ 'Cause there's noth - ing, there's

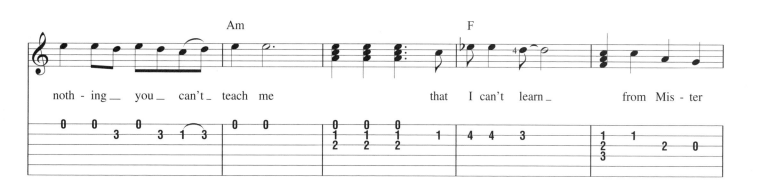

noth - ing __ you _ can't _ teach me that I can't learn _ from Mis - ter

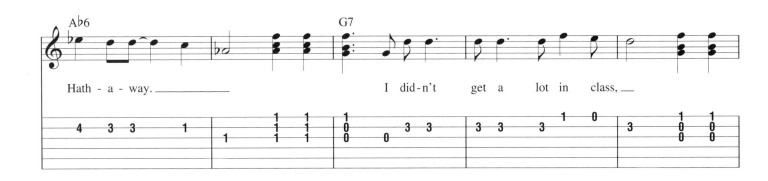

Hath - a - way. _____ I did-n't get a lot in class, ___

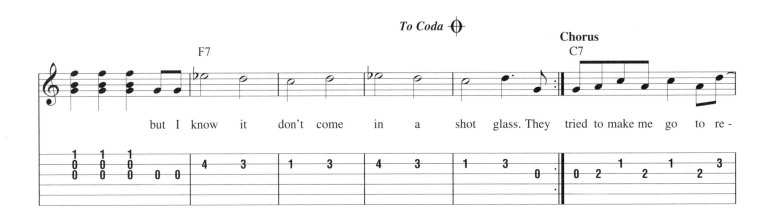

To Coda ⊕

Chorus

but I know it don't come in a shot glass. They tried to make me go to re-

- hab, _ I ___ said, ___ "No, _____ no, ____ no." ___ Yes, _ I been _ black, but when _

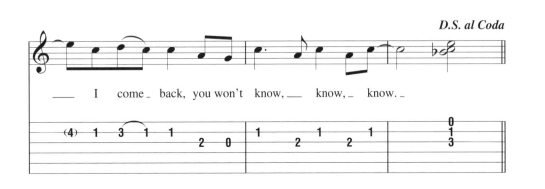

D.S. al Coda

___ I come _ back, you won't know, ___ know, _ know.

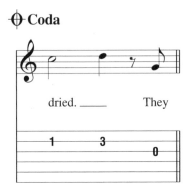

⊕ **Coda**

dried. _____ They

Outro-Chorus

tried to make me go to re - hab, I ___ said, ___ "No, ___ no, ___ no." ___ Yes, _

___ I been ___ black, but when ___ I come ___ back, you won't know, ___ know, ___ know. ___

I ain't got the time, _____ and if my dad - dy ___ thinks _ I'm _ fine, _ he's

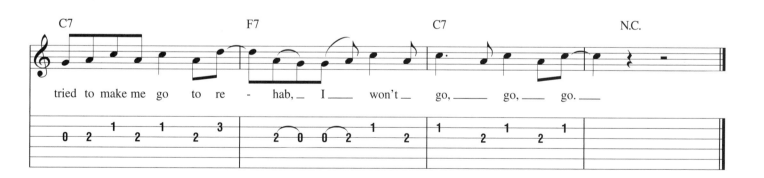

tried to make me go to re - hab, I ___ won't _ go, _____ go, ___ go. ___

Additional Lyrics

2. The man said, "Why you think you're here?"
   I said, "I got no idea."
   I'm gonna, I'm gonna lose my baby,
   So I always keep a bottle near."
   Said, "I just think you're depressed,
   Kiss me, baby, and go rest."

3. I won't ever want to drink again.
   I just, ooh, I just need a friend.
   I'm not gonna spend ten weeks,
   Have everyone think I'm on the mend.
   It's not just my pride,
   It's just 'til these tears have dried.

Rolling in the Deep

Words and Music by Adele Adkins and Paul Epworth

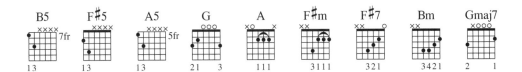

Strum Pattern: 1
Pick Pattern: 5

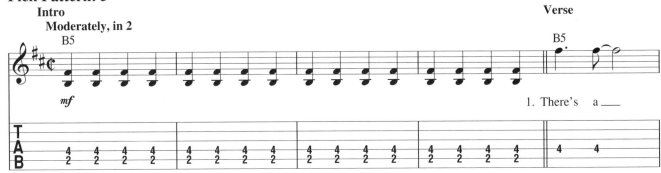

*Optional: To match recording, place capo at 1st fret.

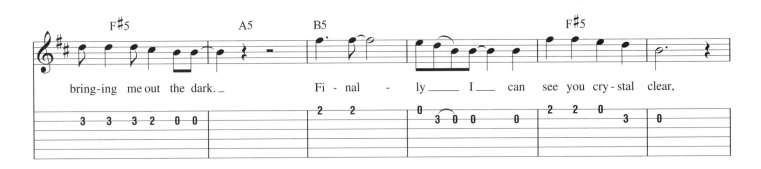

*4th verse, N.C.(Bm), next 16 meas.

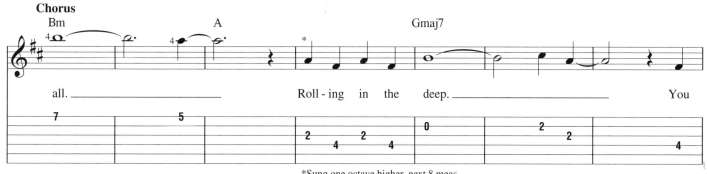

*Sung one octave higher, next 8 meas.

had my heart in - side _____ of your hand, __ and you played _ it to the beat.

We could have had it all. __

Roll-ing in the deep. _____ You had my heart in - side _____ of your hand, ____

*Sung one octave higher, next 8 meas.

D.S. al Coda

Coda
Bridge

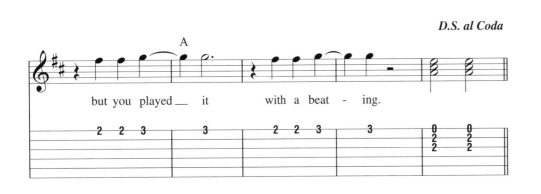

but you played _ it with a beat - ing.

(You're gon-na wish you _

**Notation in Bridge is a composite of background and lead vocals.

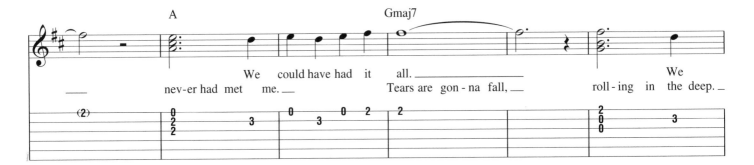

We could have had it all. _____ Tears are gon-na fall, __ We
nev-er had met me. __ roll-ing in the deep. __

146

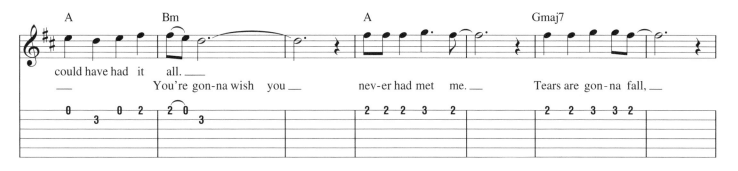

could have had it all. ___ You're gon-na wish you ___ nev-er had met me. ___ Tears are gon-na fall, ___

Outro-Chorus

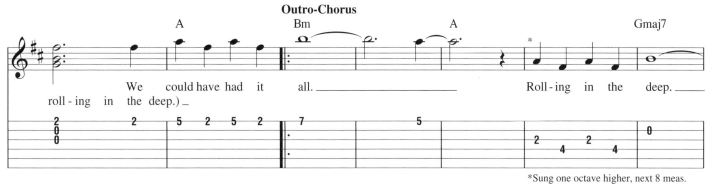

We could have had it all. _____ Roll-ing in the deep. ___
roll - ing in the deep.) _

*Sung one octave higher, next 8 meas.

You had my heart in - side _____ of your hand, _

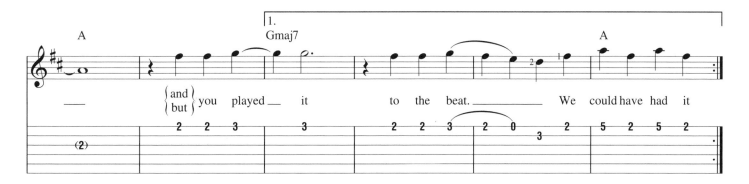

___ (and/but) you played ___ it to the beat. _____ We could have had it

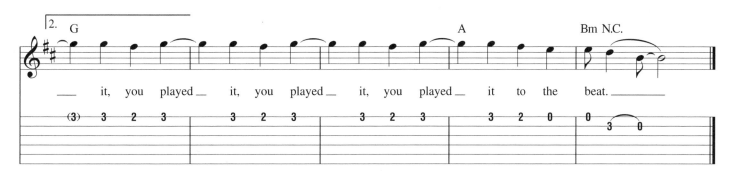

___ it, you played ___ it, you played ___ it, you played ___ it to the beat. _____

Additional Lyrics

3. Baby, I have no story to be told,
   But I've heard one on you,
   Now I'm gonna make your head burn.
   Think of me in the depths of your despair,
   Make a home down there,
   As mine sure won't be shared.

4. Throw your soul through every open door,
   Count your blessings
   To find what you look for.
   Turn my sorrows into treasured gold.
   You'll pay me back in kind,
   And reap just what you've sown.

Sailing

Words and Music by Christopher Cross

*Capo IX

Strum Pattern: 1
Pick Pattern: 5

Intro
Moderately slow, in 2

*Optional: To match recording, place capo at 9th fret.

Verse

1. Well, it's not far down to par-
   far to nev-er nev-
   not far back to san-

- a- dise, at least it's not for me, and if the
- er- land, no rea- son to pre- tend, and if the
- i- ty, at least it's not for me, and if the

wind is right you can sail a- way and find tran- quil- i- ty.
wind is right you can find the joy of in- no- cence a- gain.
wind is right you can sail a- way and find se- ren- i- ty.

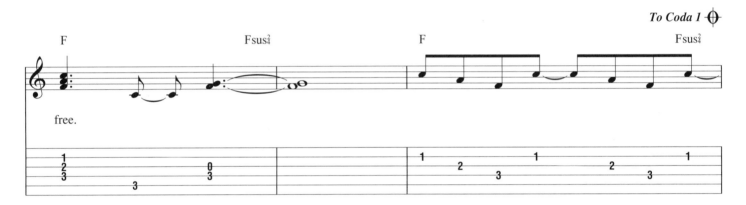

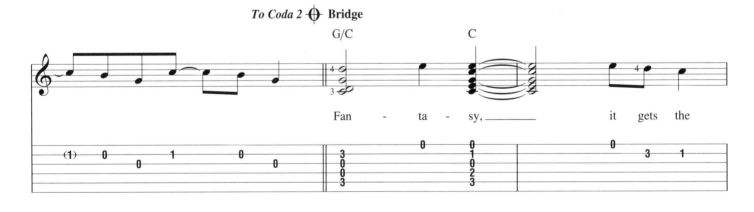

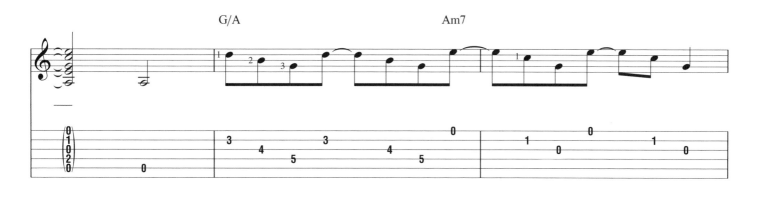

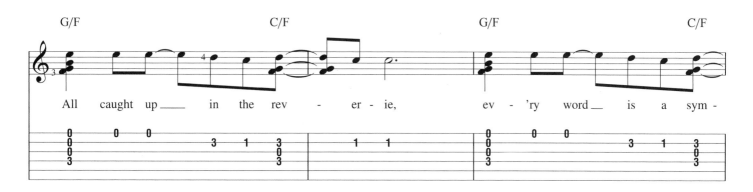

All caught up ____ in the rev - er - ie, ev - 'ry word ___ is a sym -

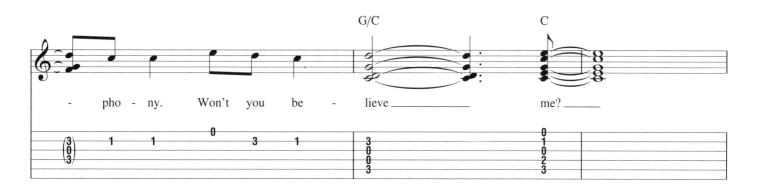

- pho - ny. Won't you be - lieve _____ me? _____

D.S. al Coda 1   ⊕ **Coda 1**   *D.S.S. al Coda 2*
(take 2nd ending)

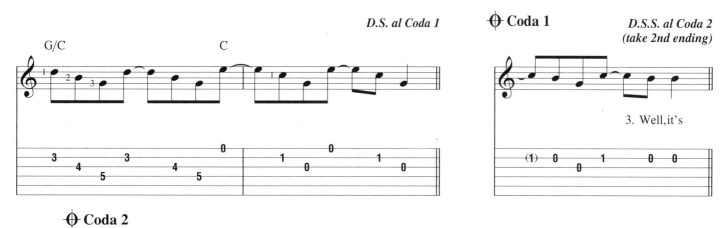

3. Well, it's

⊕ **Coda 2**

Outro

151

Smooth

Words by Rob Thomas
Music by Rob Thomas and Itaal Shur

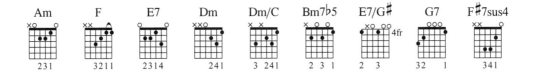

Am   F   E7   Dm   Dm/C   Bm7♭5   E7/G♯   G7   F♯7sus4

Strum Pattern: 2, 3
Pick Pattern: 3, 4

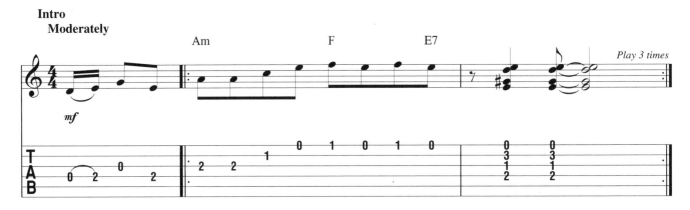

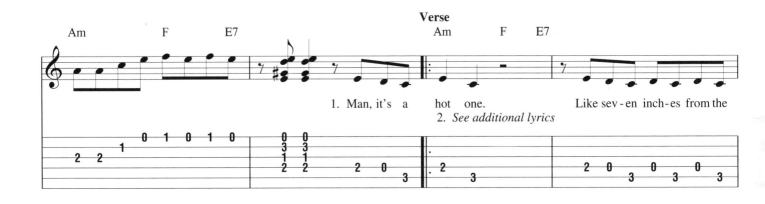

1. Man, it's a hot one.   Like sev-en inch-es from the
2. *See additional lyrics*

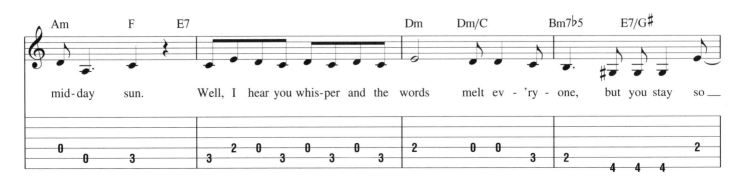

mid-day   sun.   Well, I hear you whis-per and the words   melt ev-'ry - one,   but you stay   so

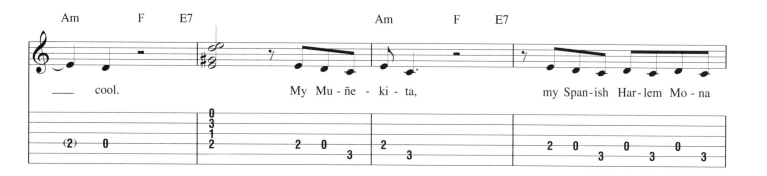

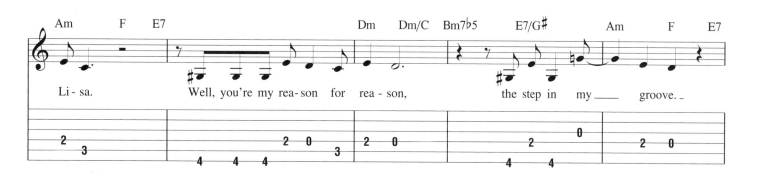

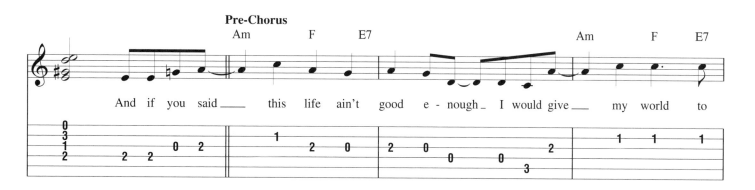

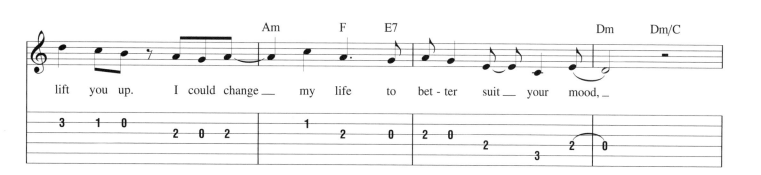

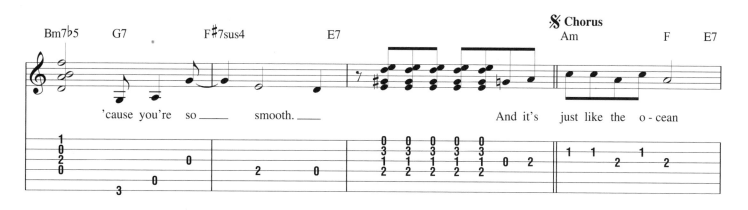

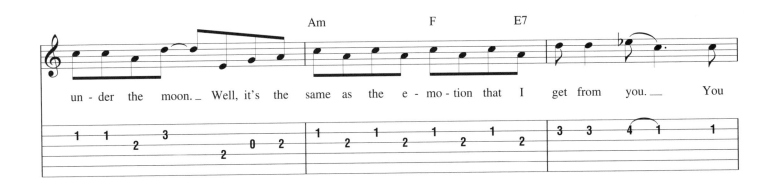

un - der the moon.___ Well, it's the same as the e - mo - tion that I get from you.___ You

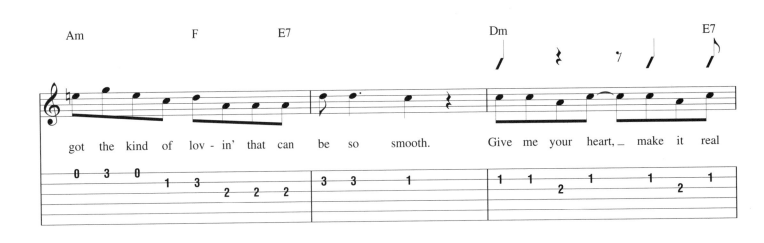

got the kind of lov - in' that can be so smooth. Give me your heart,___ make it real

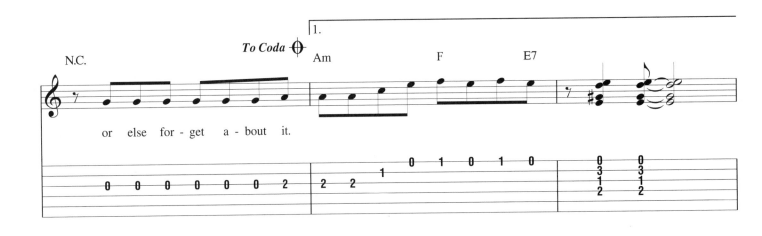

or else for - get a - bout it.

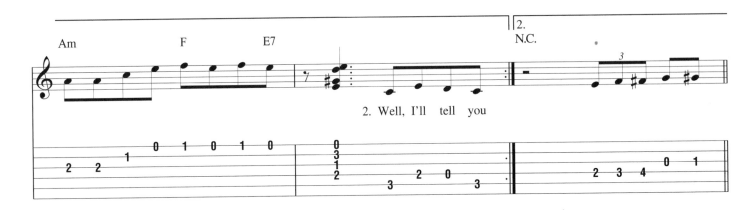

2. Well, I'll tell you

Guitar Solo

D.S. al Coda

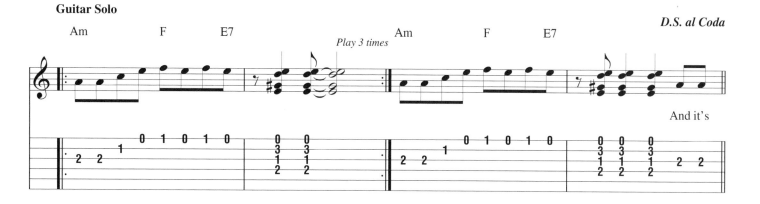

And it's

Coda
Outro

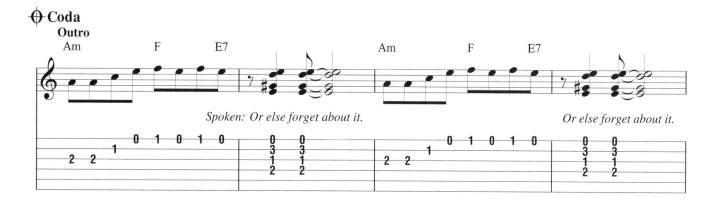

Spoken: Or else forget about it.

Or else forget about it.

Let's don't forget about it. Give me your heart, _ make it real. _

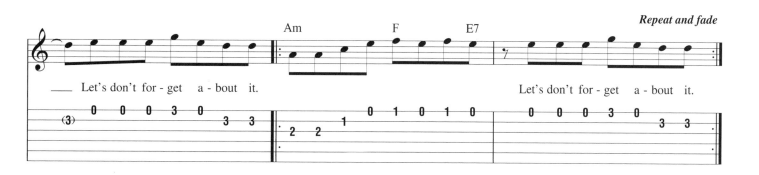

_ Let's don't for - get a - bout it.

Repeat and fade

Let's don't for - get a - bout it.

Additional Lyrics

2. Well, I'll tell you one thing,
   If you would leave it'd be a crying shame.
   In ev'ry breath and ev'ry word,
   I hear your name calling me out.
   Out from the barrio,
   You hear my rhythm on your radio.
   You feel the turning of the world so soft and slow,
   Turning me 'round and 'round.

Strangers in the Night

Words by Charles Singleton and Eddie Snyder
Music by Bert Kaempfert

Strum Pattern: 3
Pick Pattern: 3

Verse
Moderately slow

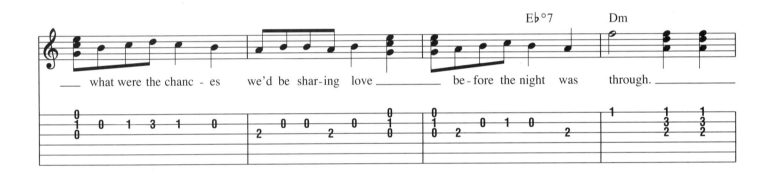

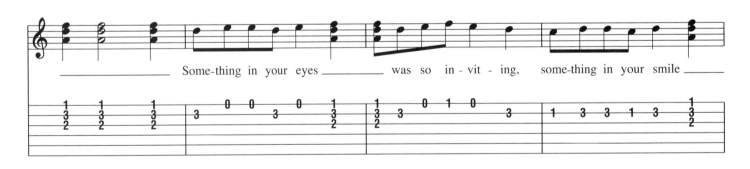

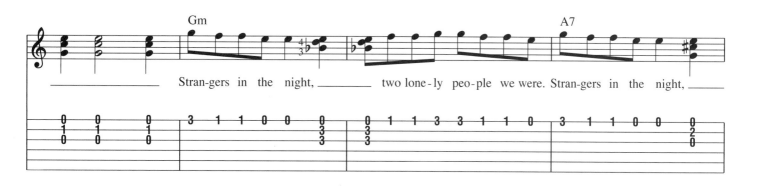

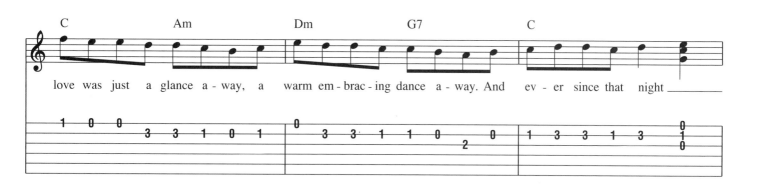

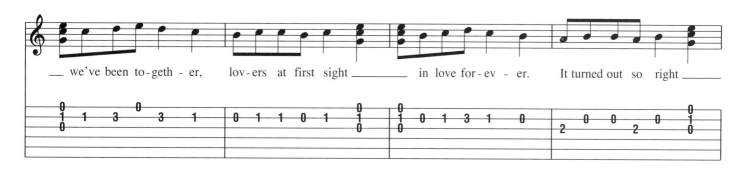

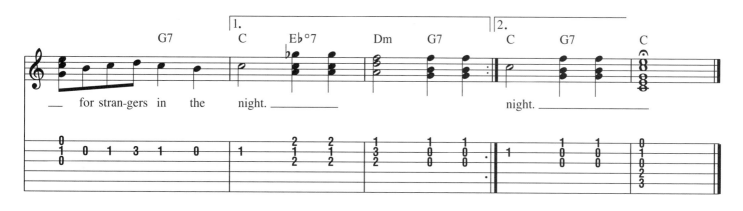

(Theme From)
A Summer Place

Words by Mack Discant
Music by Max Steiner

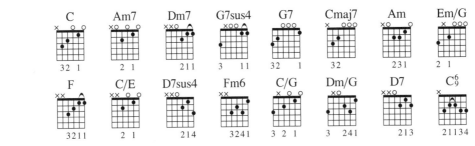

*Capo V

Strum Pattern: 8
Pick Pattern: 8

Intro
Slow, in 2

Bells will be ring - ing and birds will be sing - ing if you and your lov - er should

*Optional: To match recording, place capo at 5th fret.

Verse

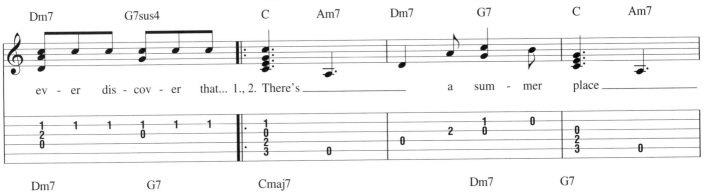

ev - er dis - cov - er that... 1., 2. There's _____ a sum - mer place _____

_____ where it may rain _____ or storm. _____ Yet I'm

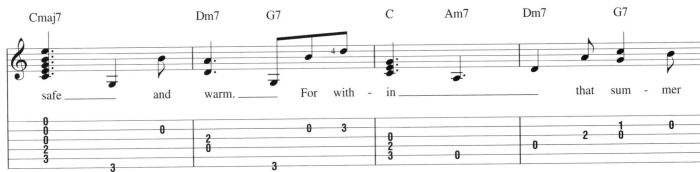

safe _____ and warm. _____ For with - in _____ that sum - mer

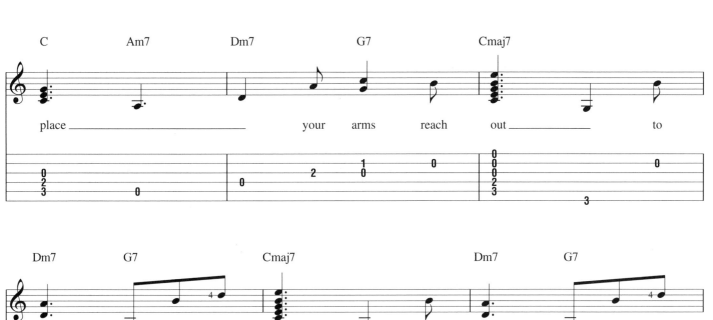

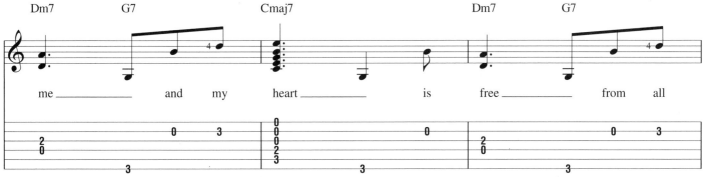

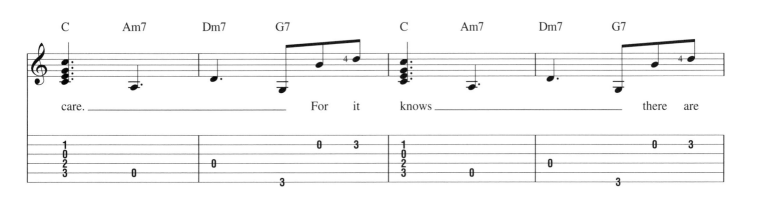

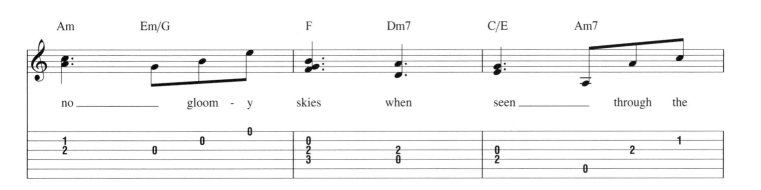

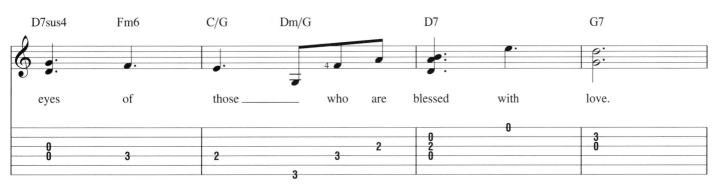

Sunny Came Home

Words and Music by Shawn Colvin and John Leventhal

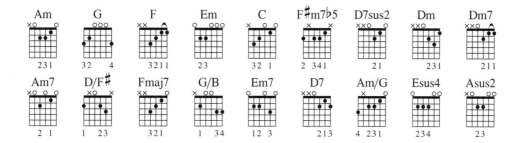

Strum Pattern: 2
Pick Pattern: 2

Intro
Moderately slow

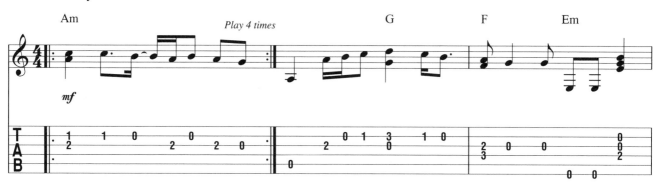

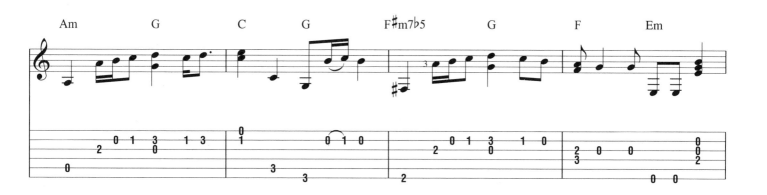

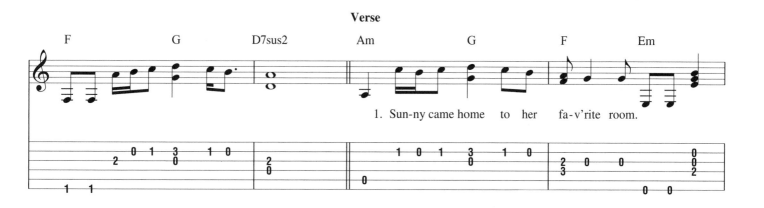

1. Sun-ny came home to her fa-v'rite room.

Sun-ny sat down in the kitch-en. She o-pened a book and a

box of tools. Sun-ny came home with a mis-sion. She says, "Days

𝄋 Chorus

go by, I'm hyp - no - tized.
I don't know why. I'm walk - ing on a wire.

To Coda ⊕

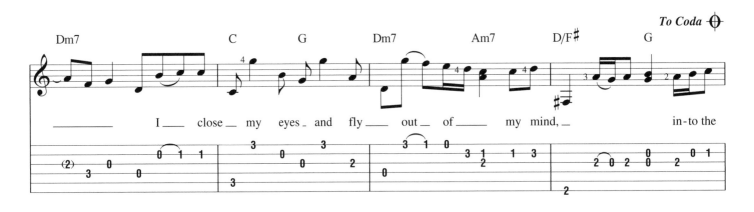

I close my eyes and fly out of my mind, in-to the

Interlude

fire."

Verse

2. Sun-ny came home with a list of names. _

She did-n't be-lieve in tran-scend-ence. "Well, it's time for a few small re-

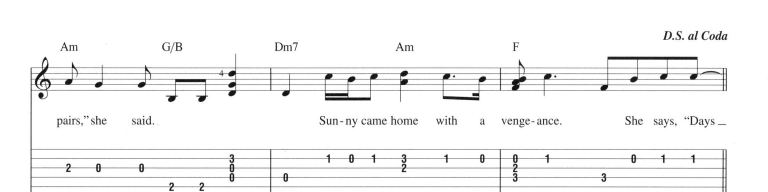

D.S. al Coda

pairs," she said. Sun-ny came home with a venge-ance. She says, "Days _

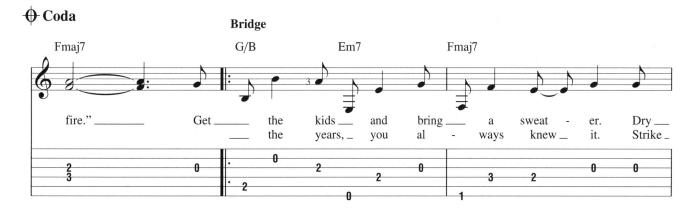

⊕ Coda

Bridge

fire." _____ Get _____ the kids _ and bring _ a sweat - er. Dry _

_____ the years, _ you al - ways knew _ it. Strike _

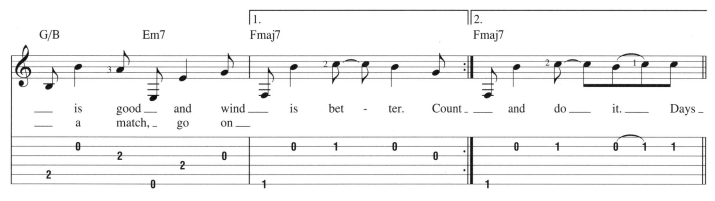

1.

2.

_ is good _ and wind _ is bet - ter. Count _ and do _ it. _ Days _

_ a match, _ go on

Chorus

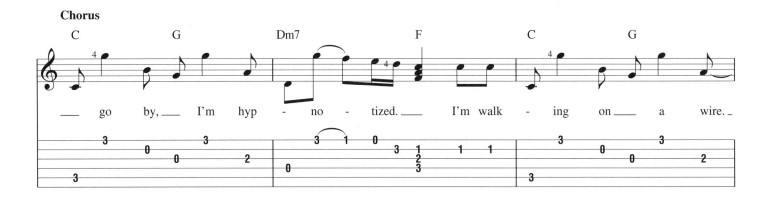

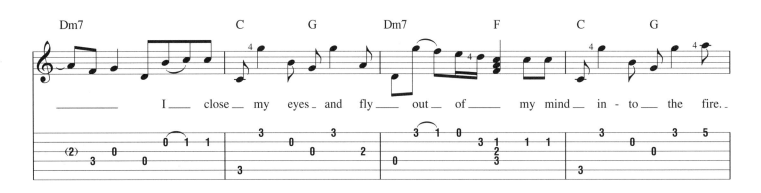

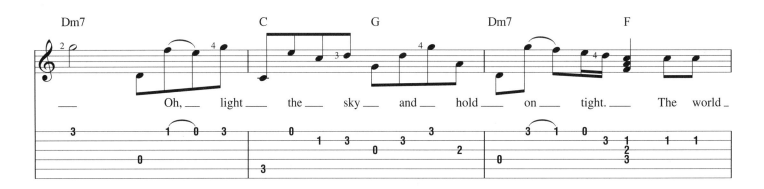

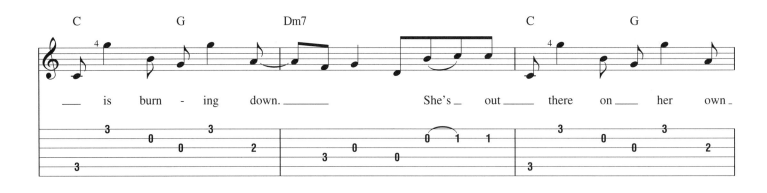

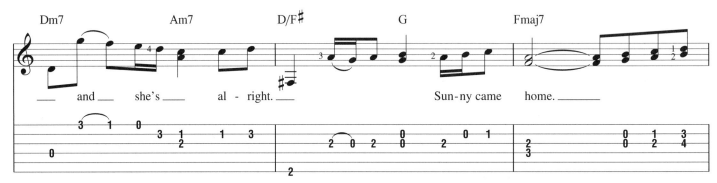

Sun - ny came

Outro

home.

Came home. _

*Tie into beat 1.

A Taste of Honey

Words by Ric Marlow
Music by Bobby Scott

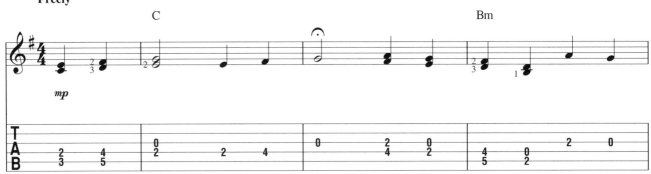

*Capo I

Strum Pattern: 1
Pick Pattern: 1

Intro
Freely

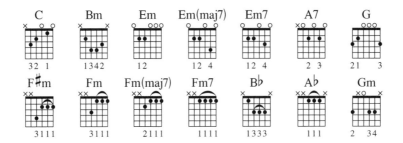

*Optional: To match recording, place capo at 1st fret.

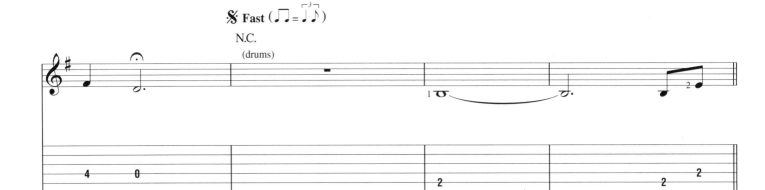

A

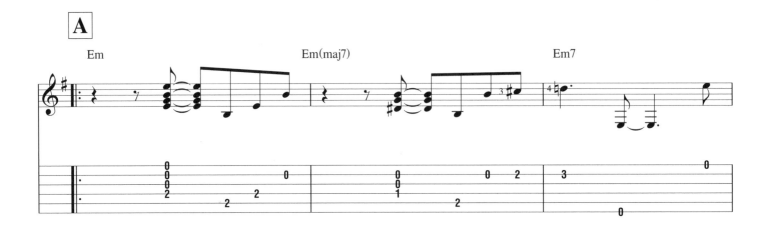

Tears in Heaven

Words and Music by Eric Clapton and Will Jennings

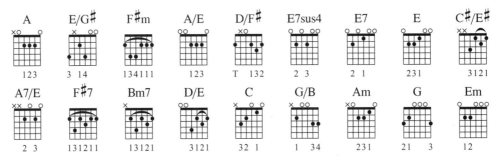

Strum Pattern: 3, 4
Pick Pattern: 3, 4

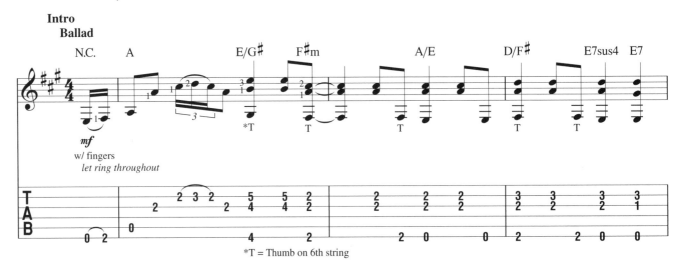

*T = Thumb on 6th string

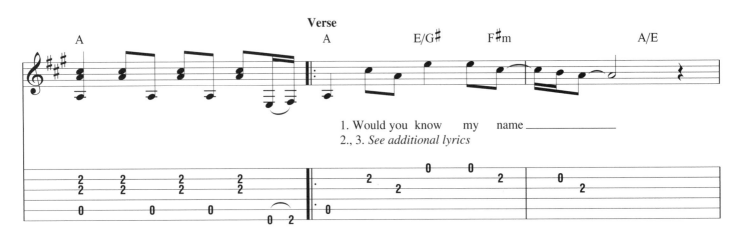

1. Would you know my name _____
2., 3. *See additional lyrics*

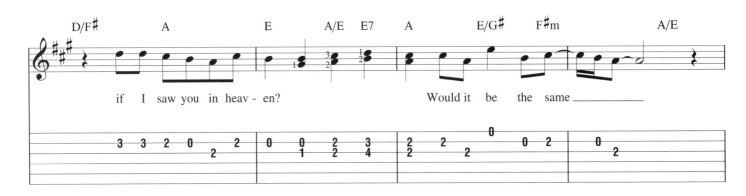

if I saw you in heav-en? Would it be the same _____

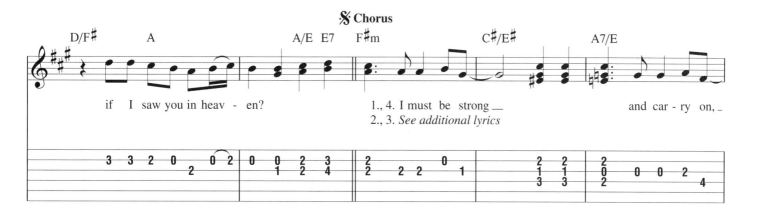

Chorus

if I saw you in heav - en?
1., 4. I must be strong ___ and car - ry on, ___
2., 3. *See additional lyrics*

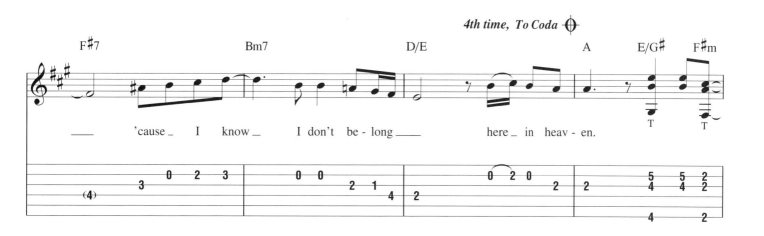

4th time, To Coda

___ 'cause ___ I know ___ I don't be - long ___ here ___ in heav - en.

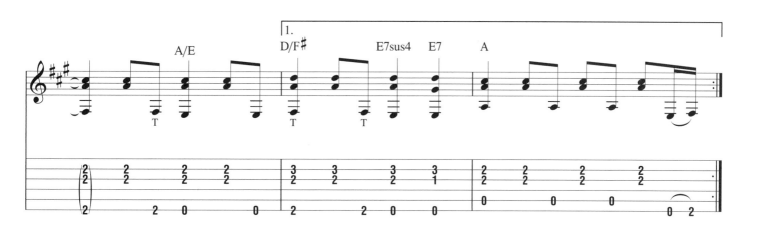

1.

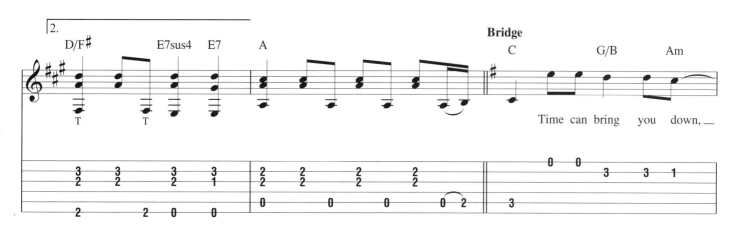

2.

Bridge

Time can bring you down, ___

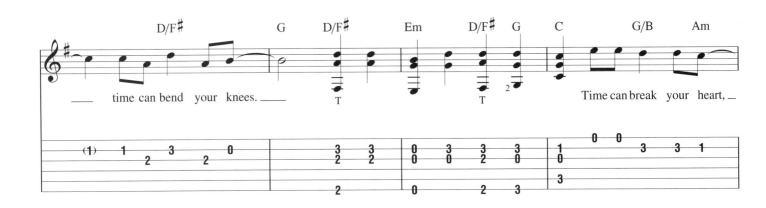

time can bend your knees. _____ Time can break your heart, _____

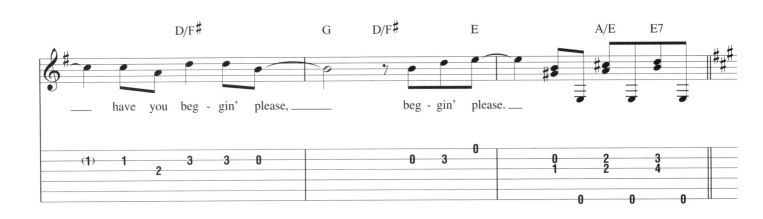

have you beg-gin' please, _____ beg-gin' please. _____

Interlude

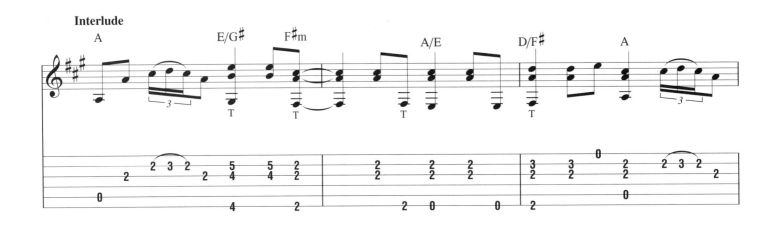

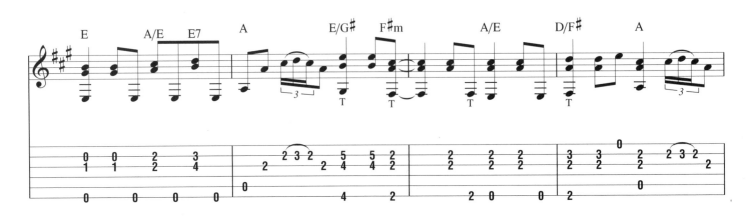

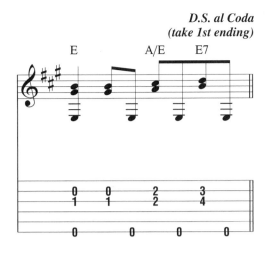
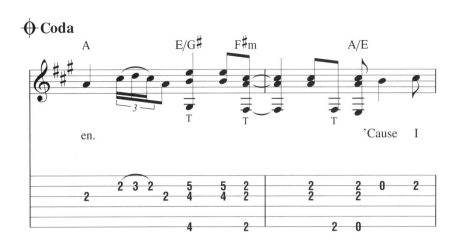

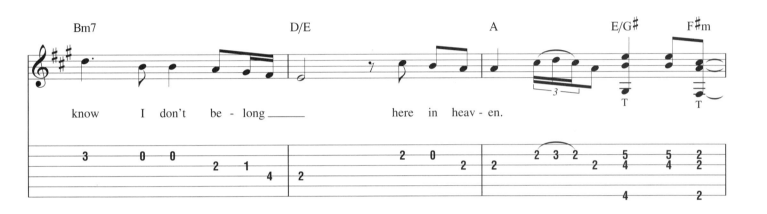

Additional Lyrics

2. Would you hold my hand
   If I saw you in heaven?
   Would you help me stand
   If I saw you in heaven?

3. Would you know my name
   If I saw you in heaven?
   Would you be the same
   If I saw you in heaven?

Chorus 2. I'll find my way
   Through night and day
   'Cause I know I just can't stay
   Here in heaven.

Chorus 3. Beyond the door
   There's peace, I'm sure,
   And I know there'll be no more
   Tears in heaven.

This Masquerade

Words and Music by Leon Russell

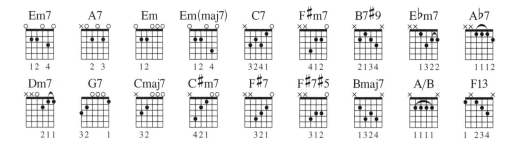

*Capo I

Strum Pattern: 5
Pick Pattern: 4

Intro-Guitar Solo
Moderately slow

Verse

** *Play 5 times*

1. Are we real - ly hap -
2nd time, Piano solo

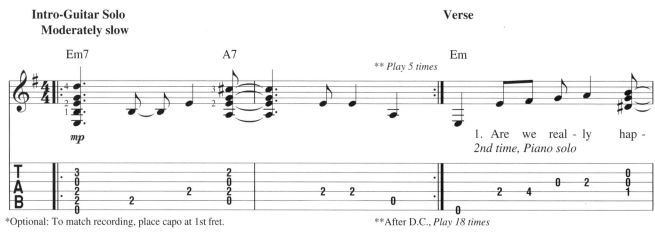

*Optional: To match recording, place capo at 1st fret.

**After D.C., *Play 18 times*

- py here ___ with this lone - ly game we play,

look - ing for words _____ to say?

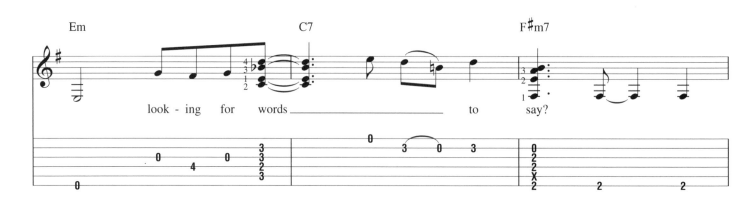

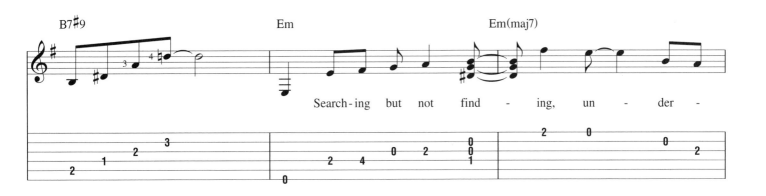

Searching but not finding, under-

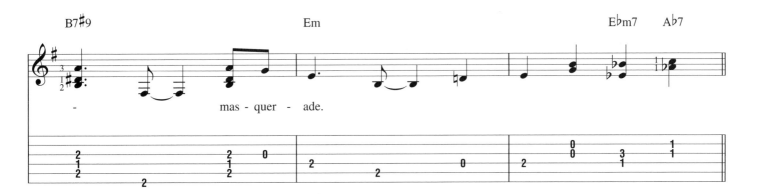

standing anyway, we're lost in a mas-

masquerade.

Bridge

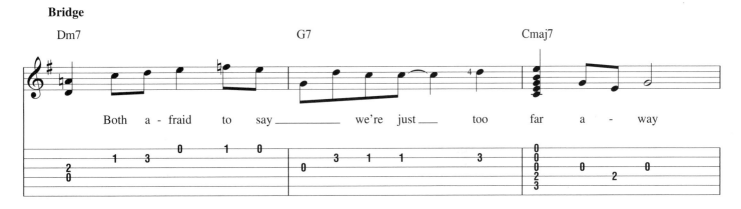

Both afraid to say we're just too far away

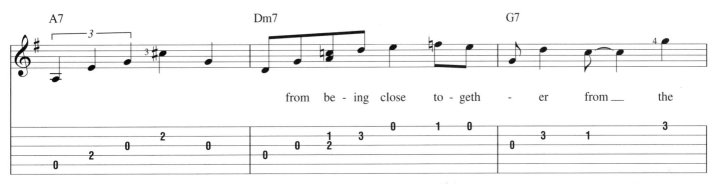

from being close together from the

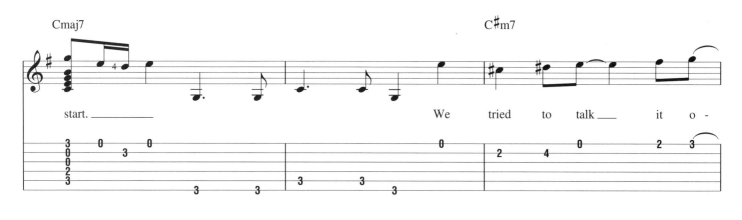

start. _____ We tried to talk _____ it o-

-ver, but the words _____ got in _____ the _____ way. _____ We're

lost in - side _____ this lone - ly game _____ we play. _

Verse

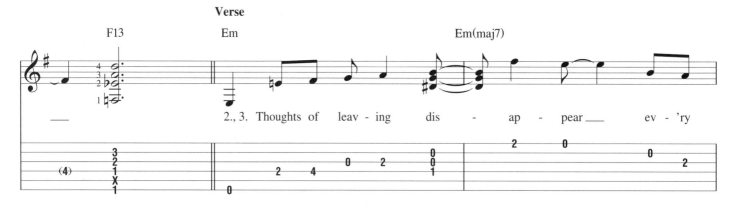

_____ 2., 3. Thoughts of leav-ing dis - ap - pear _____ ev-'ry

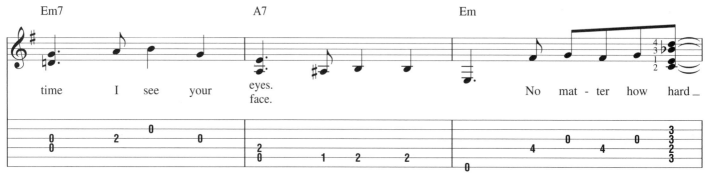

time I see your eyes.
face. No mat-ter how hard _

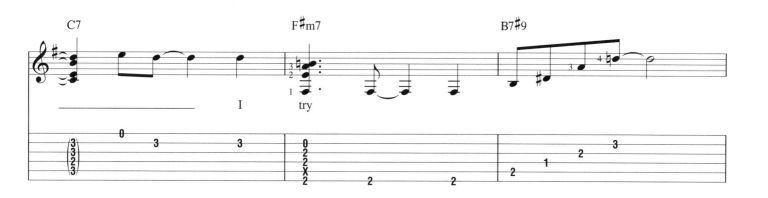

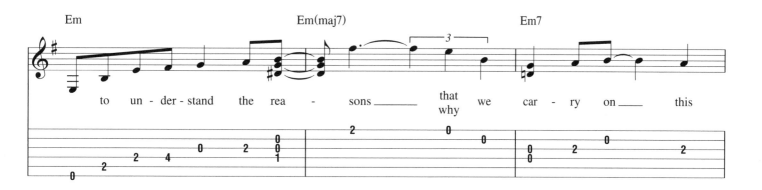

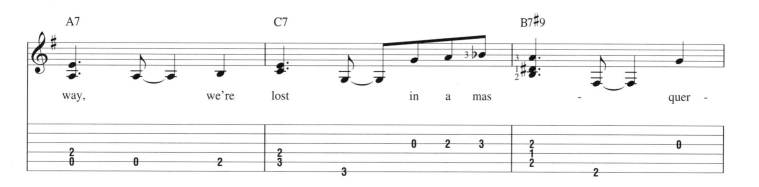

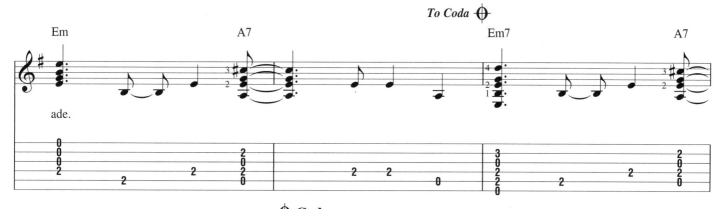

To Coda ⊕

⊕ **Coda**

D.C. al Coda
(take repeat)

Outro-Guitar Solo

Repeat and fade

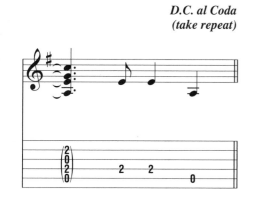

Unforgettable

Words and Music by Irving Gordon

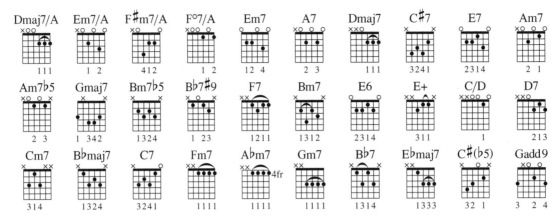

*Capo III

Strum Pattern: 3
Pick Pattern: 3

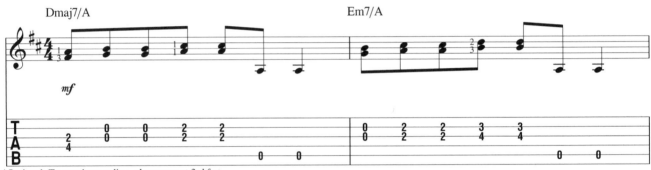

*Optional: To match recording, place capo at 3rd fret.

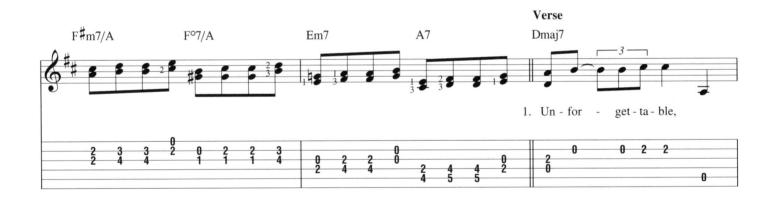

1. Un - for - get - ta - ble,

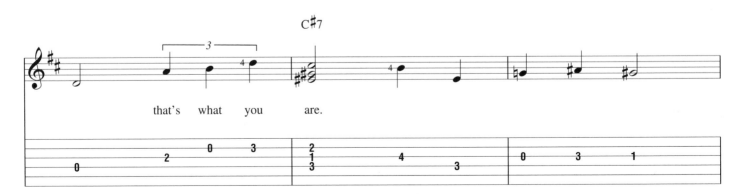

that's what you are.

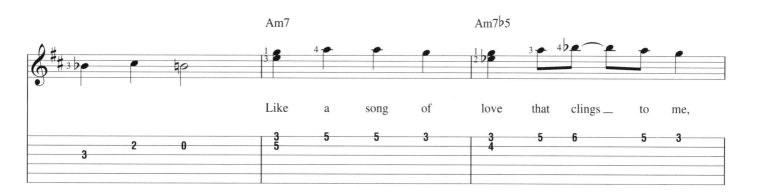

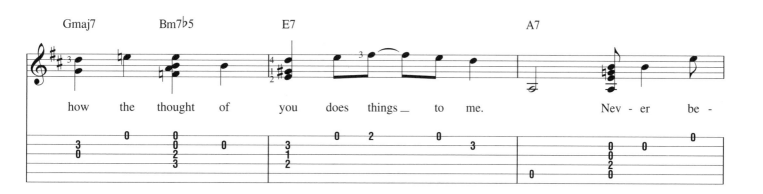

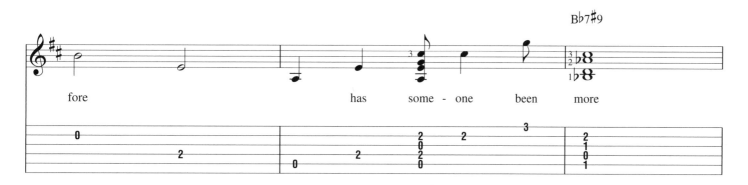

and for - ev - er - more,   that's how you'll   stay.

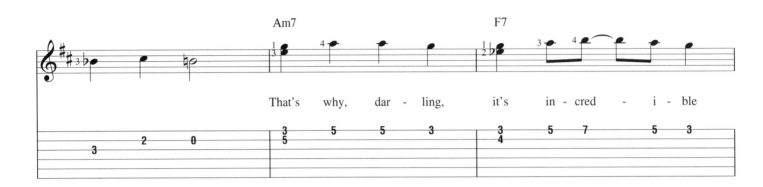

That's   why,   dar - ling,   it's   in - cred - i - ble

To Coda ⊕

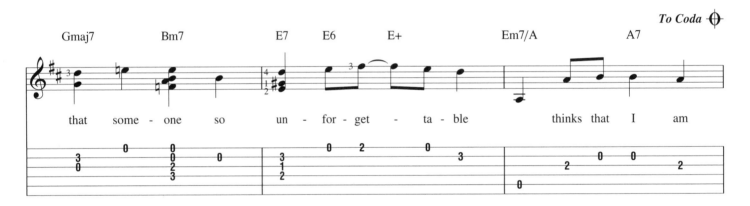

that   some - one   so   un - for - get - ta - ble   thinks that   I   am

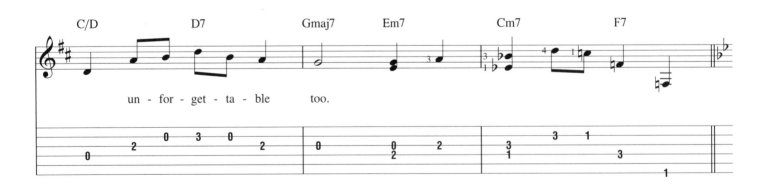

un - for - get - ta - ble   too.

Instrumental

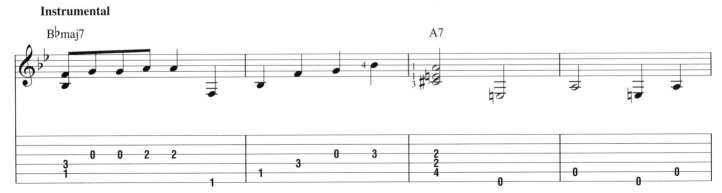

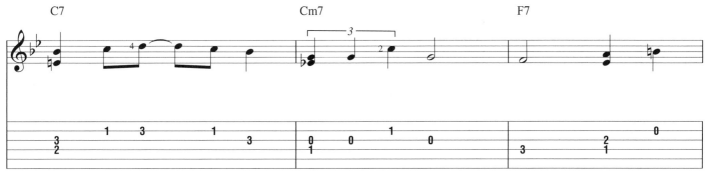

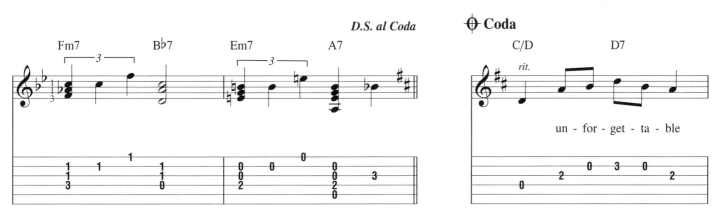

D.S. al Coda

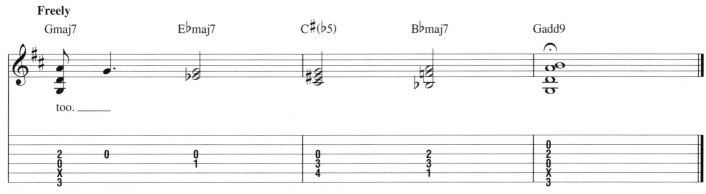

Up, Up and Away

Words and Music by Jimmy Webb

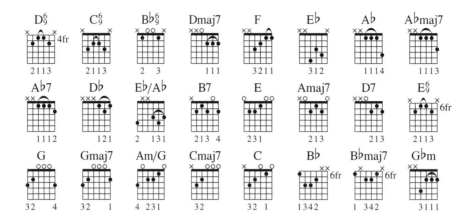

*Capo III

Strum Pattern: 2
Pick Pattern: 1

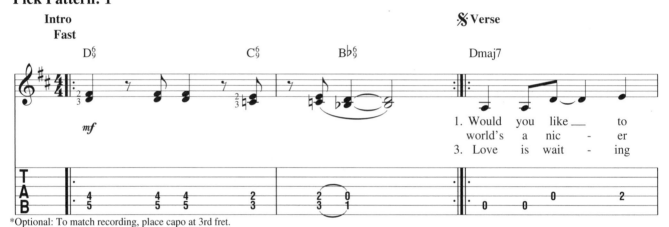

*Optional: To match recording, place capo at 3rd fret.

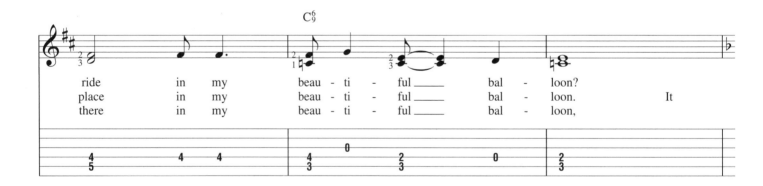

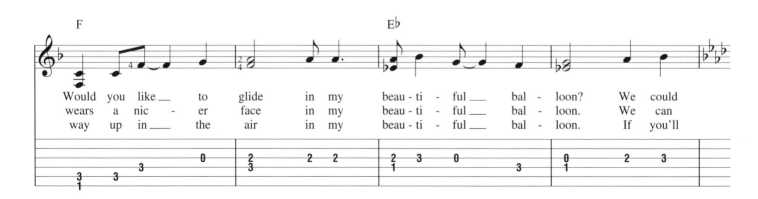

float a-mong the stars to-geth - er, you and I, ___
sing a song and sail a-long the sil - ver sky, ___ for we can
hold my hand, we'll chase your dream a - cross the sky, ___

fly! ___ We can fly! ___

Chorus

To Coda ⊕

Up, up and a-way, ___ my beau-ti-ful, ___ my beau-ti-ful ___ bal-

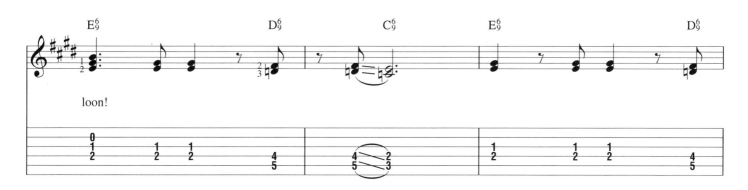

loon!

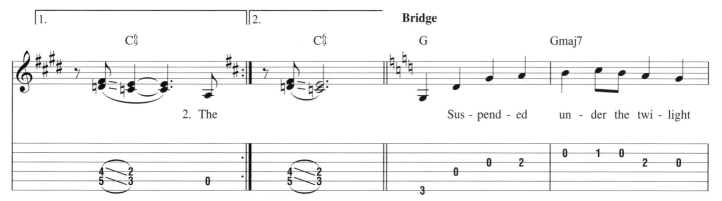

1.

2.   **Bridge**

2. The   Sus - pend - ed   un - der the twi - light

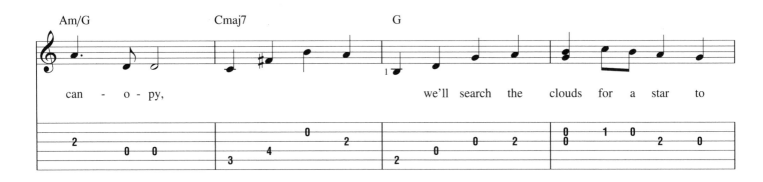

can - o - py,   we'll search the clouds for a star to

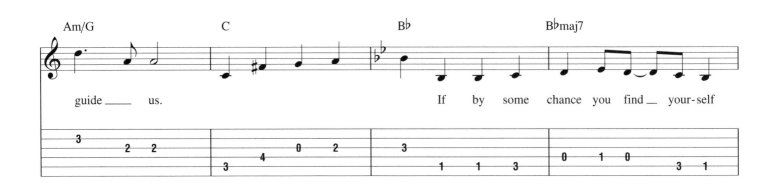

guide ___ us.   If by some chance you find ___ your-self

lov - ing me,   we'll find a cloud ___ to hide us,

D.S. al Coda   ⊕ **Coda**

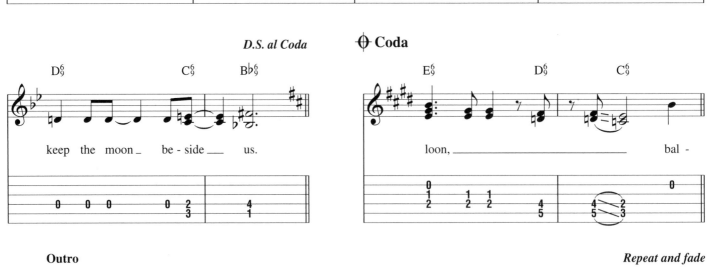

keep the moon ___ be - side ___ us.   loon, _____ bal -

Outro   *Repeat and fade*

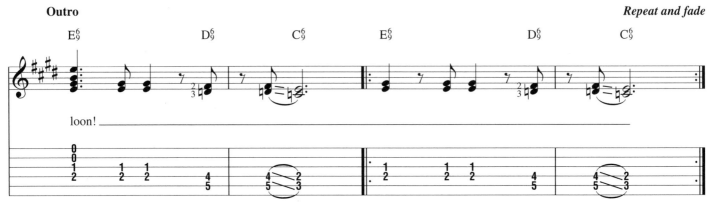

loon! _____

Walk On

Words by Bono
Music by U2
Dedicated to Aung San Suu Kyi

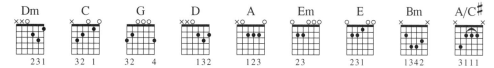

Strum Pattern: 6
Pick Pattern: 1

Intro
Moderately

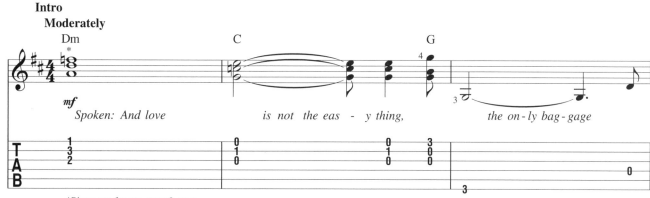

*Piano arr. for gtr., next 8 meas.

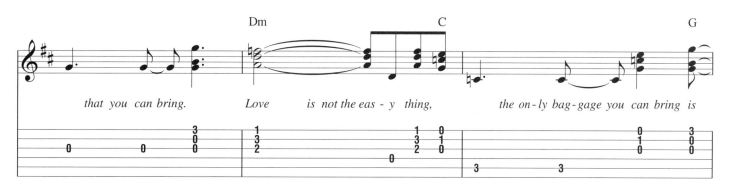

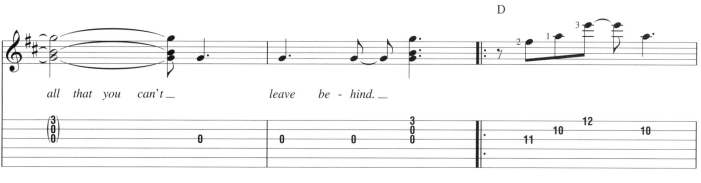

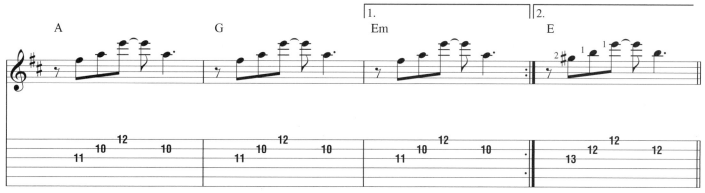

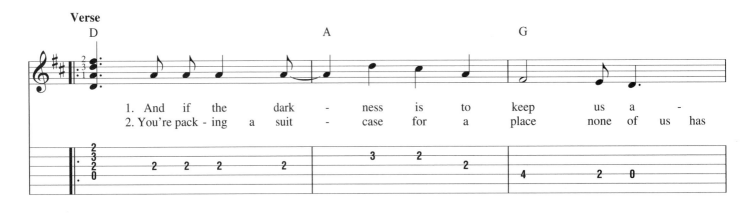

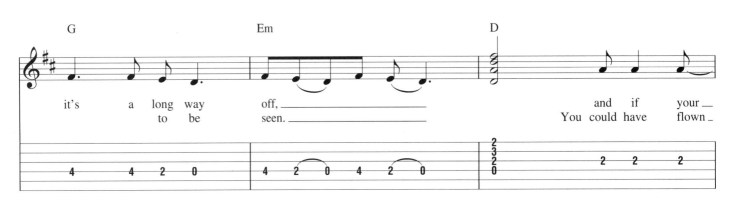

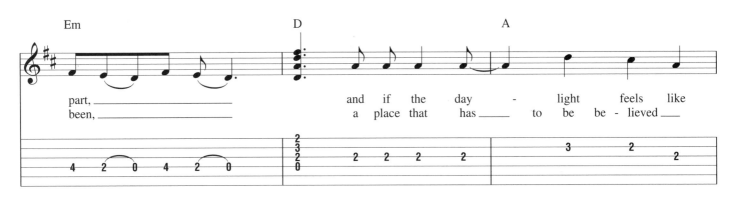

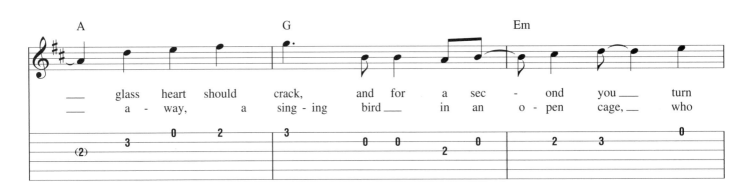

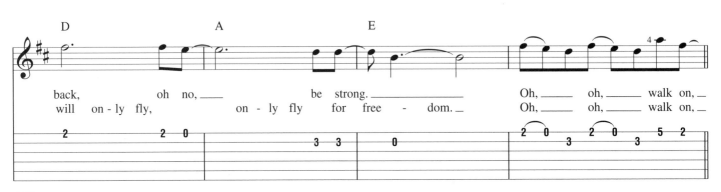

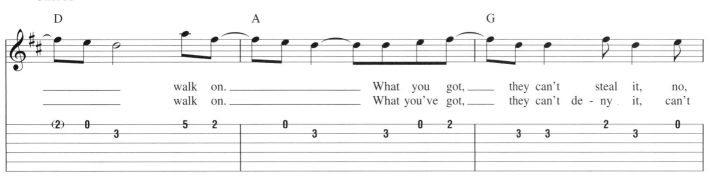

walk on. _____ What you got, _____ they can't steal it, no,
walk on. _____ What you've got, _____ they can't de - ny it, can't

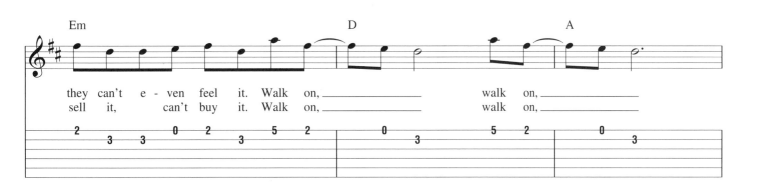

they can't e - ven feel it. Walk on, _____ walk on, _____
sell it, can't buy it. Walk on, _____ walk on, _____

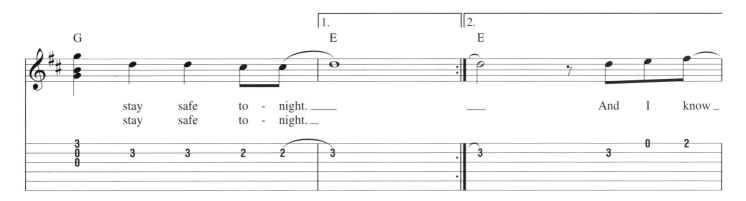

stay safe to - night. _____
stay safe to - night. _____

And I know _

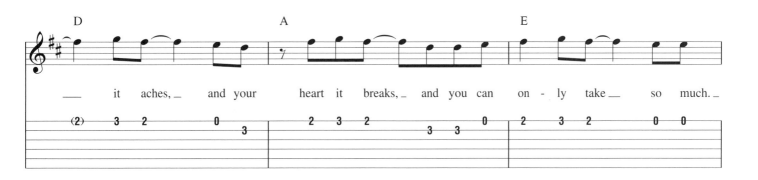

___ it aches, _ and your heart it breaks, _ and you can on - ly take _ so much. _

Guitar Solo

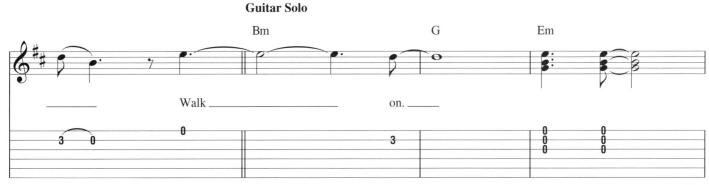

_____ Walk _____ on. _____

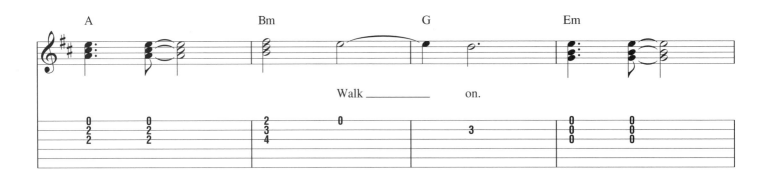

Walk _____ on.

Bridge

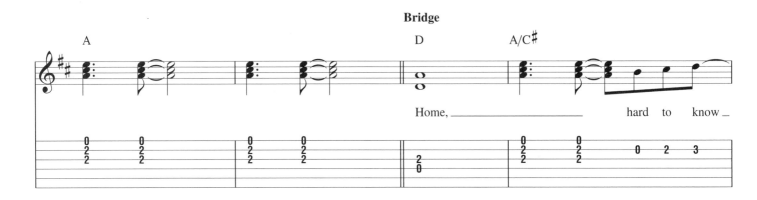

Home, _____ hard to know __

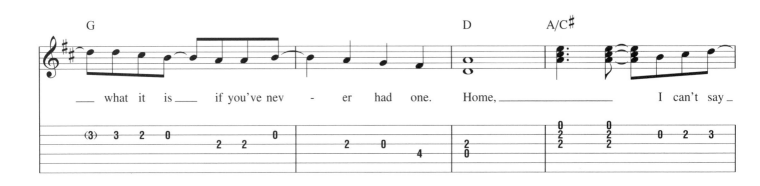

__ what it is __ if you've nev - er had one. Home, _____ I can't say

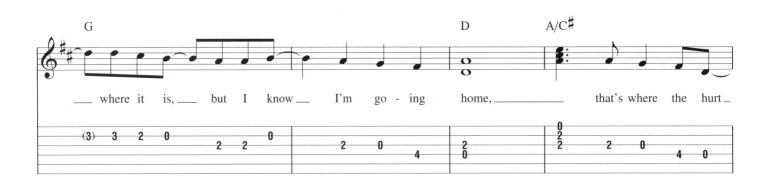

__ where it is, __ but I know __ I'm go - ing home, _____ that's where the hurt __

__ is. _____ And I know __ it aches, __ and your

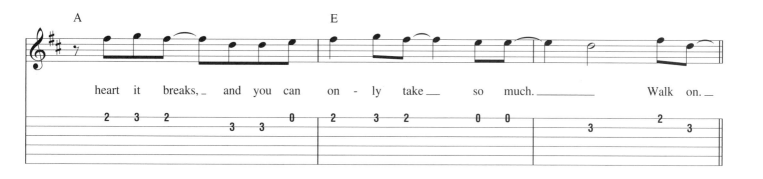

heart it breaks, __ and you can on - ly take __ so much. _____ Walk on. __

Outro

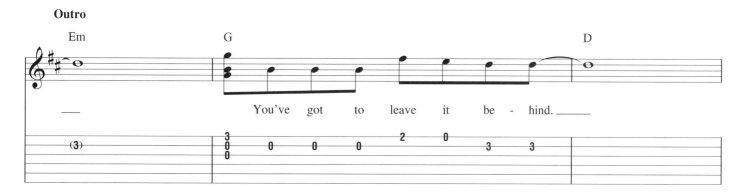

__ You've got to leave it be - hind. _____

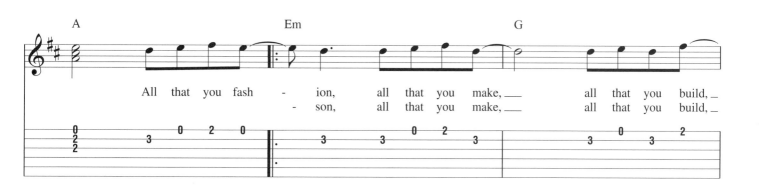

All that you fash - ion, all that you make, ___ all that you build, __
 - son, all that you make, ___ all that you build, __

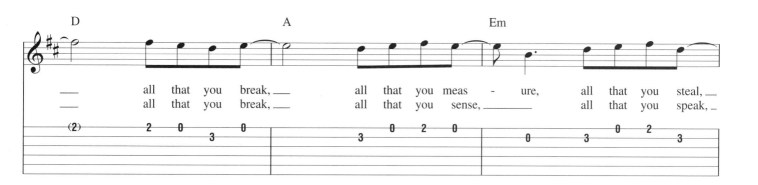

__ all that you break, ___ all that you meas - ure, all that you steal, __
__ all that you break, ___ all that you sense, _____ all that you speak, __

Repeat and fade

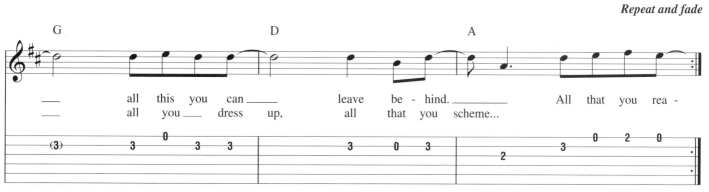

__ all this you can ___ leave be - hind. _____ All that you rea -
__ all you __ dress up, all that you scheme...

Use Somebody

Words and Music by Caleb Followill, Nathan Followill, Jared Followill and Matthew Followill

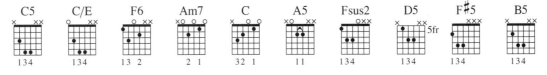

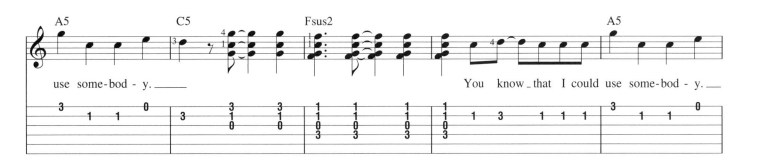

use some-bod - y. _____ You know _ that I could use some-bod - y. __

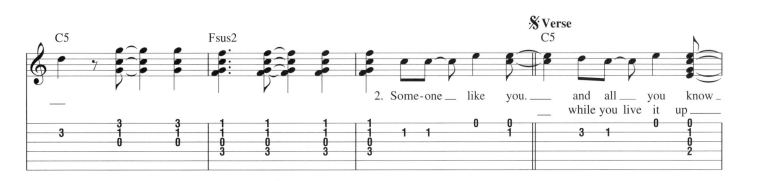

𝄋 **Verse**

_ 2. Some-one _ like you. _____ and all _ you know _ while you live it up _____

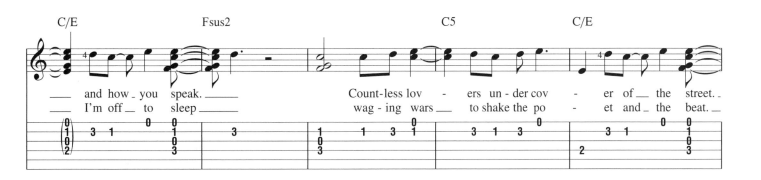

_____ and how _ you speak. _____ Count-less lov - ers un - der cov - er of _ the street. _
_____ I'm off _ to sleep _____ wag - ing wars _____ to shake the po - et and _ the beat. _

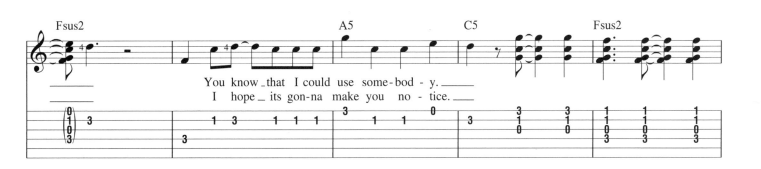

You know _ that I could use some-bod - y. _____
I hope _ its gon-na make you no - tice. _____

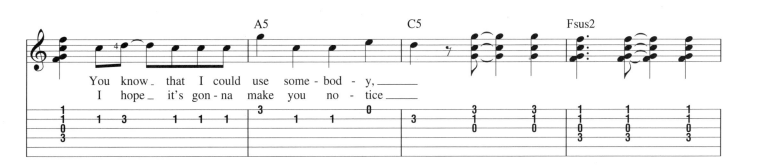

You know _ that I could use some-bod - y, _____
I hope _ it's gon - na make you no - tice _____

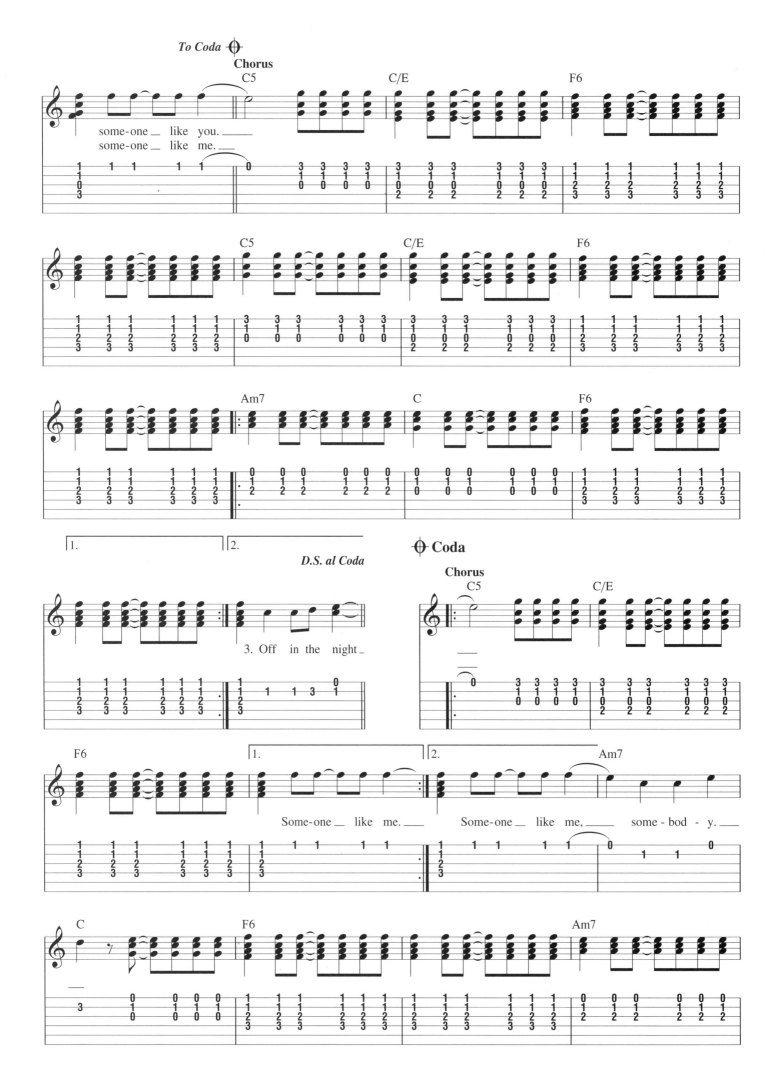

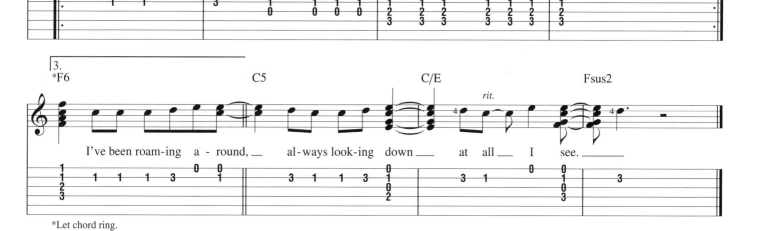

*Let chord ring.

Volare

Music by Domenico Modugno
English Lyric by Mitchell Parish
Original Italian Text by Domenico Modugno and Francesco Migliacci

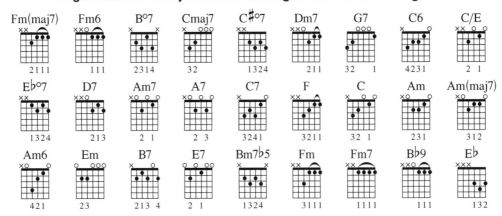

*Tune down 1 step:
(low to high) D-G-C-F-A-D

Strum Pattern: 3
Pick Pattern: 3

Intro
Moderately

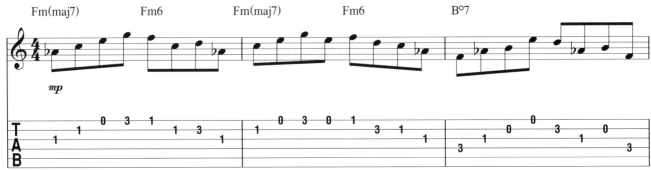

*Optional: To match recording, tune down 1 step.

Verse
Freely, in 2

1. Pen - so che un so - gno co - sì non ri - tor - ni mai
2. Ma tut - ti sog - ni ne - ll'al - ba sva - nis - con per -

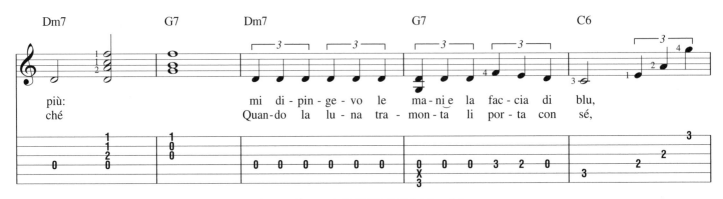

più:
ché

mi di - pin - ge - vo le ma - ni e la fac - cia di blu,
Quan - do la lu - na tra - mon - ta li por - ta con sé,

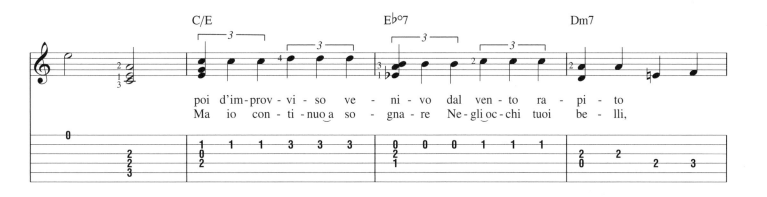

poi d'im-prov-vi-so ve-ni-vo dal ven-to ra-pi-to
Ma io con-ti-nuo a so-gna-re Ne-gli oc-chi tuoi be - lli,

e in-co-min-cia-vo a vo - la - re nel-cie-lo in-fi - ni - to.
che so-no blu Co-mo un cie-lo trap-un-to di ste - lle.

Chorus
Moderately fast (♩♩ = ♩♪)

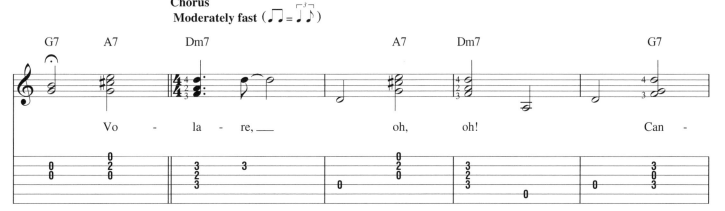

Vo - la - re, ___ oh, oh! Can -

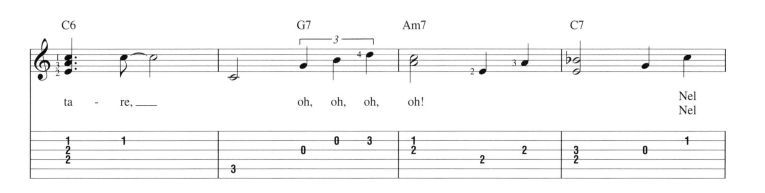

ta - re, ___ oh, oh, oh, oh! Nel / Nel

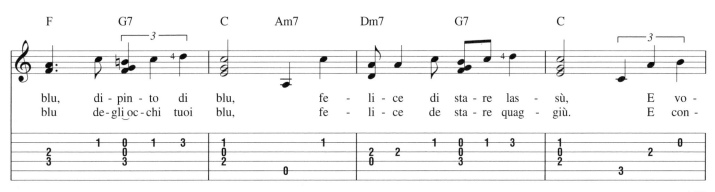

blu, di-pin-to di blu, fe - li-ce di sta-re las-sù, E vo-
blu de-gli oc-chi tuoi blu, fe - li-ce de sta-re quag-giù. E con-

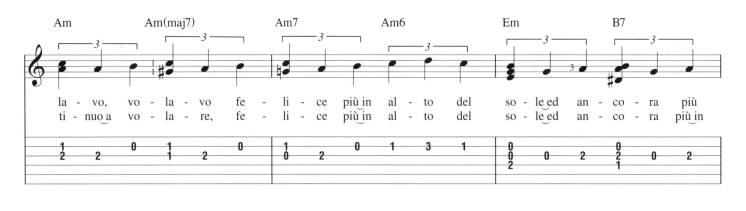

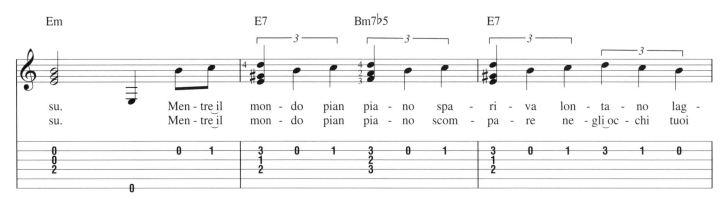

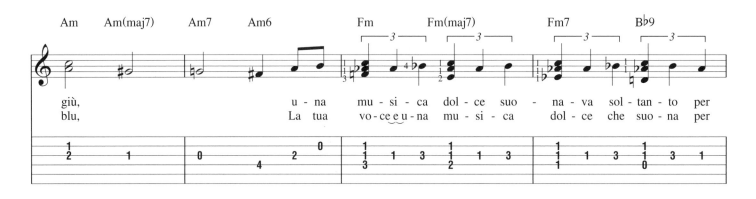

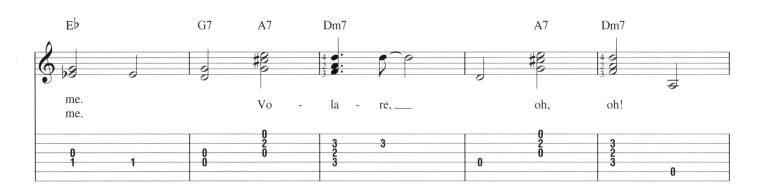

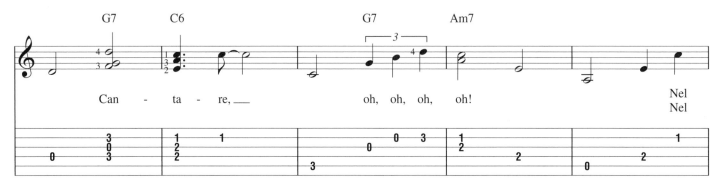

English Translation

Verse 1 I think that a dream almost never returns:
I was painting my hands and my face blue.
Then suddenly I flew, carried away by the wind,
And I began to fly into the infinite sky.

Chorus 1 To fly, oh, oh! To sing, oh, oh, oh, oh!
In the blue, painted blue, happy to stay up there.
And I flew, I flew,
Happy in the heights of the sun and beyond.
While the world very slowly disappeared below,
A sweet music played only for me.
To fly, oh, oh! To sing, oh, oh, oh, oh!
In the blue, painted blue, happy to stay up there.

Verse 2 But all of the dreams vanish at dawn because
When the moon is setting, it brings them with it.
But I continue to dream in your beautiful eyes,
Which are blue like a sky patterned with stars.

Chorus 2 To fly, oh, oh! To sing, oh, oh, oh, oh!
In the blue of your blue eyes, happy to stay on earth.
And I continue to fly,
Happy in the heights of the sun and beyond.
While the world very slowly disappears in your blue eyes,
Your voice is a sweet music that sounds for me.
To fly, oh, oh! To sing, oh, oh, oh, oh!
In the blue of your blue eyes, happy to stay on earth.
In the blue of your blue eyes, happy to stay on earth.

English Lyrics

Verse 1, 2 Sometimes the world is a valley of heartaches and tears,
And in the hustle and bustle no sunshine appears.
But you and I have our love always there to remind us,
There is a way we can leave all the shadows behind us.

Chorus 1 Volare, oh, oh! Cantare, oh, oh, oh, oh!
Let's fly way up to the clouds,
Away from the maddening crowds
We can sing in the glow of a star that I know of,
Where lovers enjoy peace of mind.
Let us leave the confusion and all disillusion behind.
Just like birds of a feather, a rainbow together we'll find.
Volare, oh, oh! Cantare, oh, oh, oh, oh!
No wonder my happy heart sings,
Your love has given me wings.

Chorus 2 Volare, oh, oh! Cantare, oh, oh, oh, oh!
Let's fly way up to the clouds,
Away from the maddening crowds
We can sing in the glow of a star that I know of,
Where lovers enjoy peace of mind.
Let us leave the confusion and all disillusion behind.
Just like birds of a feather, a rainbow together we'll find.
Volare, oh, oh! Cantare, oh, oh, oh, oh!
No wonder my happy heart sings,
Your love has given me wings.
Your love has given me wings.
Your love has given me wings.

We Are the World

Words and Music by Lionel Richie and Michael Jackson

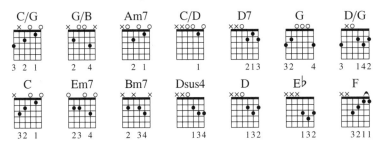

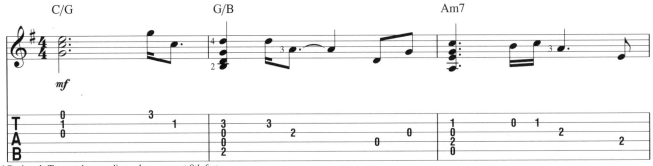

*Capo IX

Strum Pattern: 4
Pick Pattern: 4

Intro
Moderately slow

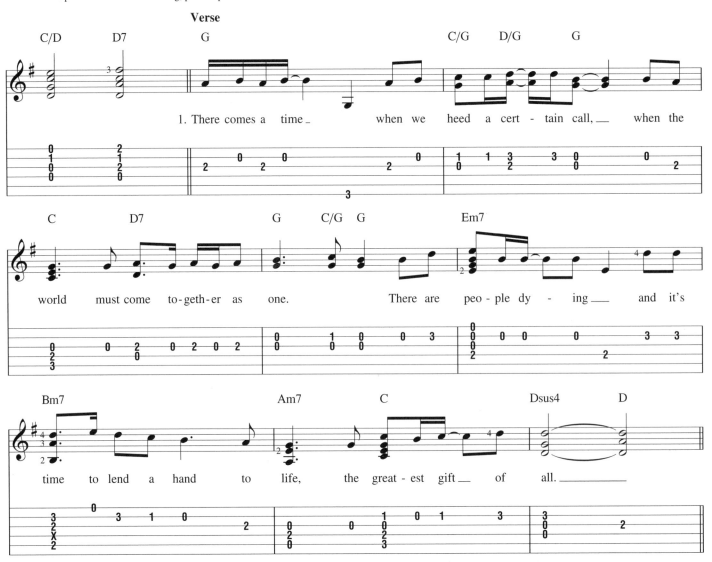

*Optional: To match recording, place capo at 9th fret.

Verse

1. There comes a time ___ when we heed a cert - tain call, ___ when the world must come to-geth-er as one. There are peo - ple dy - ing ___ and it's time to lend a hand to life, the great - est gift ___ of all. ___

Verse

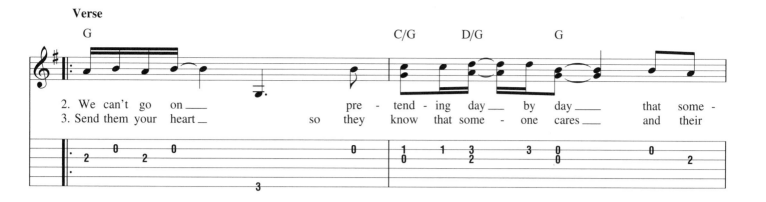

2. We can't go on ___ pre - tend - ing day __ by day ___ that some -
3. Send them your heart __ so they know that some - one cares ___ and their

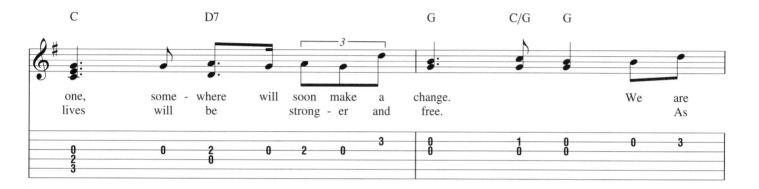

one, some - where will soon make a change. ___ We are
lives will be strong - er and free. ___ As

all a part ___ of _____ God's great big fam - i - ly and the
God has shown _ us _____ by turn - ing stone __ to bread, so we

Chorus

truth, _ you know, love is all __ we need. _____ We are the world, we are the
all __ must lend a help - ing hand. _____

*Lyrics sung one octave higher throughout Chorus & Bridge.

chil - dren, we are the ones ___ to make a bright - er day, so let's __ start

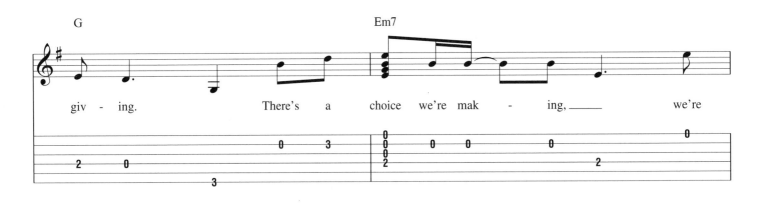

giv - ing.   There's   a   choice   we're   mak - ing, _____   we're

sav - ing   our ___   own   lives.   It's   true, ___   we   make   a   bet - ter   day,   just   you ___   and

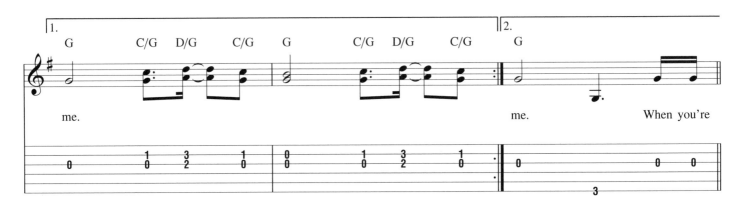

me.   me.   When you're

Bridge

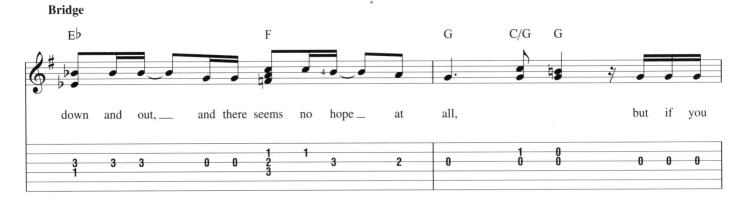

down   and   out, ___   and   there   seems   no   hope ___   at   all,   but   if   you

just   be - lieve, _   there's   no   way   we _   can   fall.   Let   us   re - al - ize, _   oh,   that   a

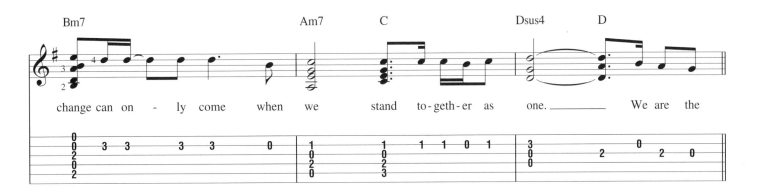

change can on - ly come when we stand to-geth-er as one. _____ We are the

Chorus

world, we are the chil - dren, we are the ones ___

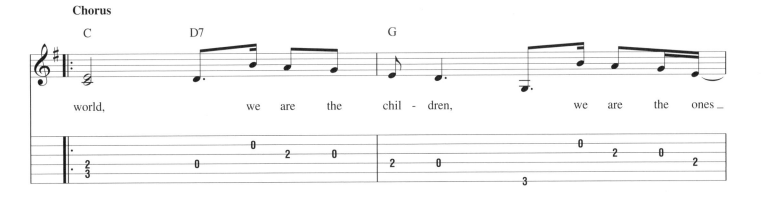

___ to make a bright - er day, so let's ___ start giv - ing. There's a

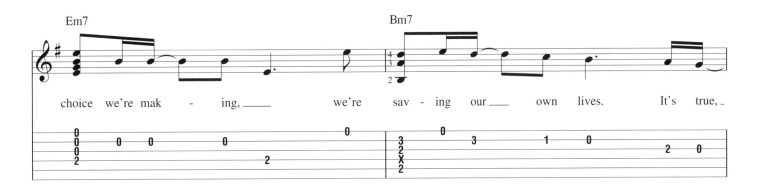

choice we're mak - ing, ___ we're sav - ing our ___ own lives. It's true, ___

Repeat and fade

___ we make a bet - ter day, just you ___ and me. We are the

What a Fool Believes

Words and Music by Michael McDonald and Kenny Loggins

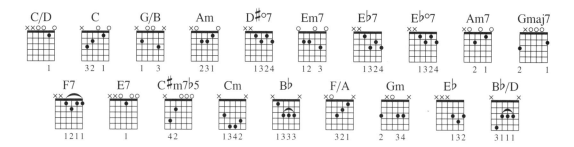

*Capo VI

Strum Pattern: 5
Pick Pattern: 1

Intro
Moderately

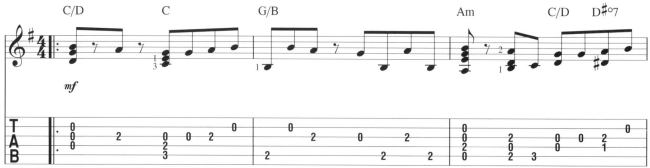

*Optional: To match recording, place capo at 6th fret.

1. He came from some-where back in her long

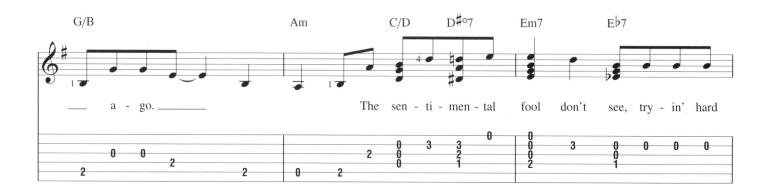

a - go. The sen-ti-men-tal fool don't see, try-in' hard

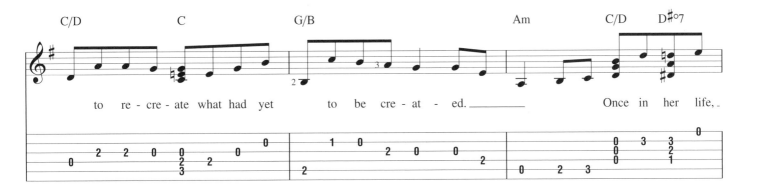

to re-cre-ate what had yet to be cre-at-ed. _____ Once in her life, _

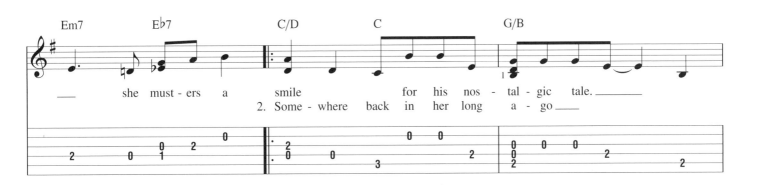

_____ she must-ers a smile for his nos - tal-gic tale. _____
2. Some - where back in her long a - go _____

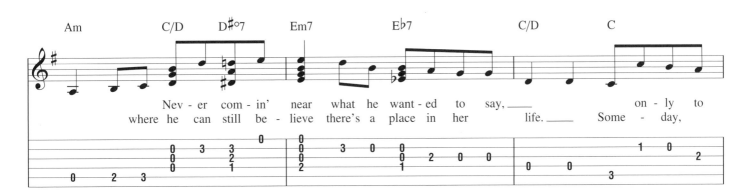

Nev - er com - in' near what he want - ed to say, _____ on - ly to
where he can still be - lieve there's a place in her life. _____ Some - day,

real - ize it nev - er real - ly was.
some - where, she will re - turn. _____

Pre-Chorus

She had a place _____ in _____ his life.

203

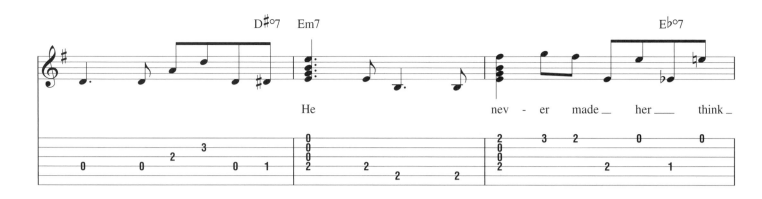

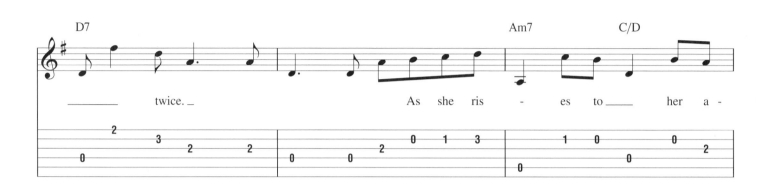

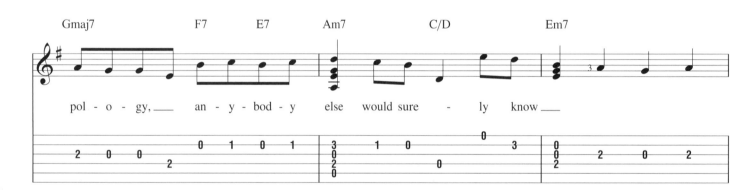

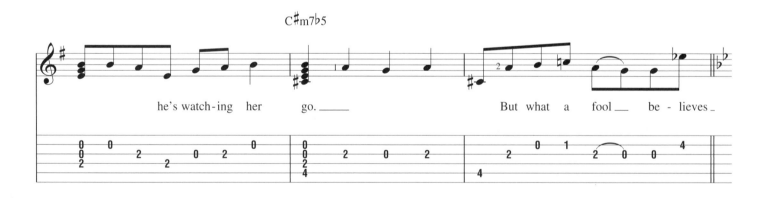

Chorus

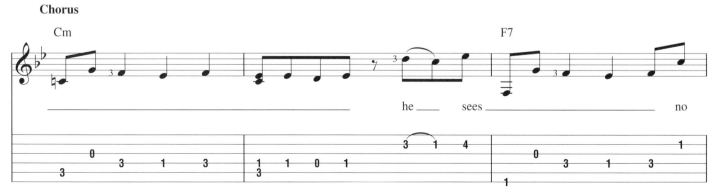

wise man has the pow - er   to rea - son a - way

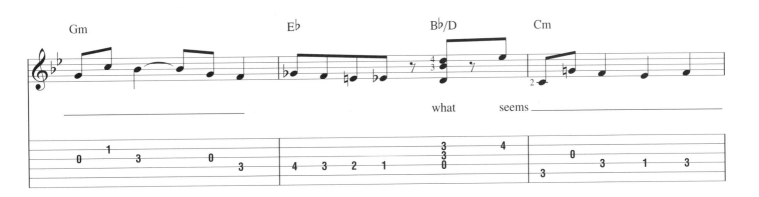

what seems

to ___ be _____ is al - ways bet - ter than noth -

ing.   1. And noth - ing at all _____
                                                 2. There's

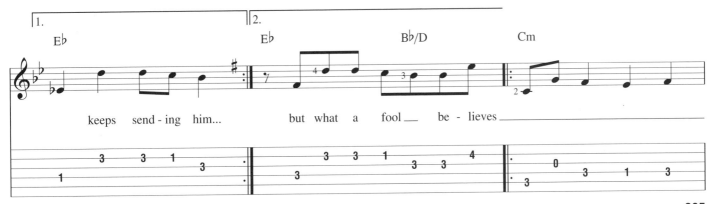

keeps send - ing him...   but what a fool ___ be - lieves _____

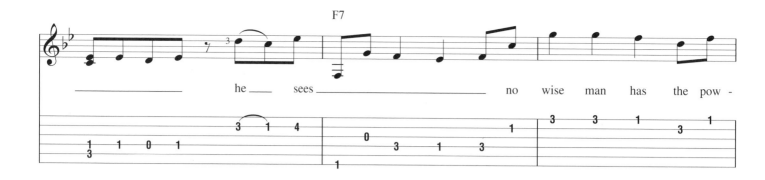

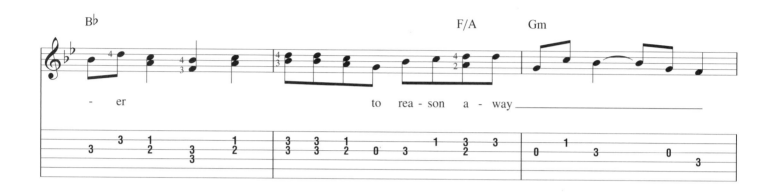

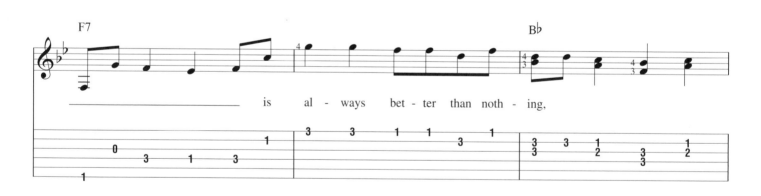

Repeat and fade

The Wind Beneath My Wings

Words and Music by Larry Henley and Jeff Silbar

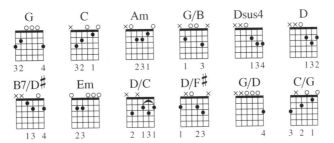

*Capo III

Strum Pattern: 4
Pick Pattern: 4

*Optional: To match recording, place capo at 3rd fret.

Verse

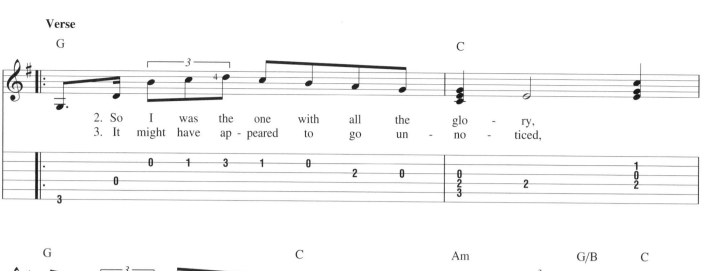

2. So I was the one with all the glo - ry,
3. It might have ap - peared to go un - no - ticed,

while you were the one with all the strength,
but I've got it all here in my heart.

a beau - ti - ful face with - out a
I want you to know I know the

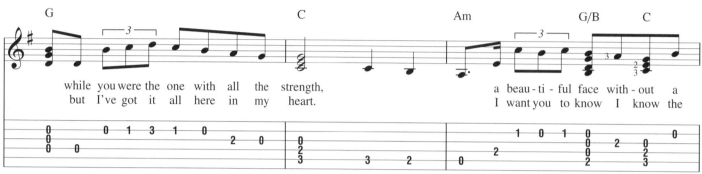

name for so long, _
truth, (of) course I know _ it:

a beau - ti - ful smile to hide the pain.
I would be noth - ing with - out you.

𝄋 Chorus

Did you ev - er know that you're my he - ro
Did you ev - er know that you're my he - ro?
Did I ev - er tell you you're my he - ro?

You're

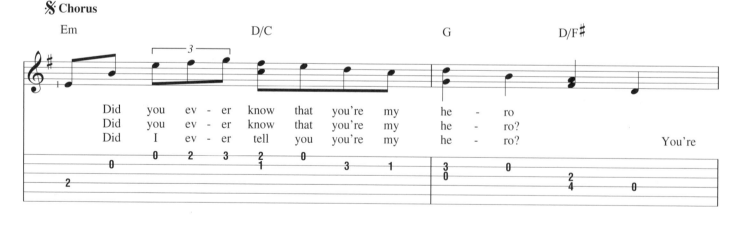

and ev - 'ry - thing I would like to _____ be?
You're ev - 'ry - thing I wish I could _____ be.
ev - 'ry - thing, ev - 'ry - thing I wish I could _____ be.

What's Love Got to Do with It

Words and Music by Terry Britten and Graham Lyle

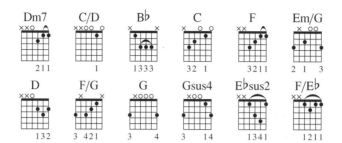

*Capo VI

Strum Pattern: 3
Pick Pattern: 3

Intro
Moderately slow

*Optional: To match recording, place capo at 6th fret.

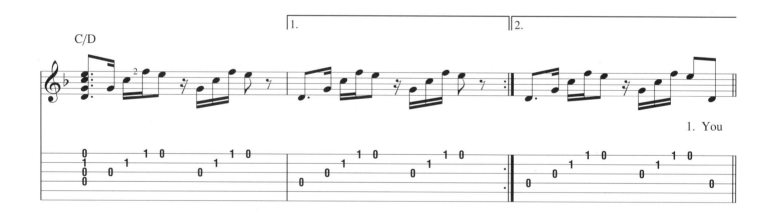

1. You

Verse

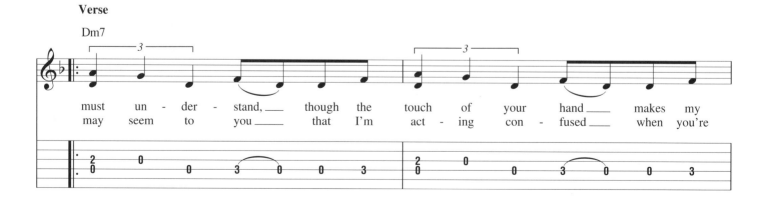

must un- der- stand,___ though the touch of your hand ___ makes my
may seem to you ___ that I'm act- ing con- fused ___ when you're

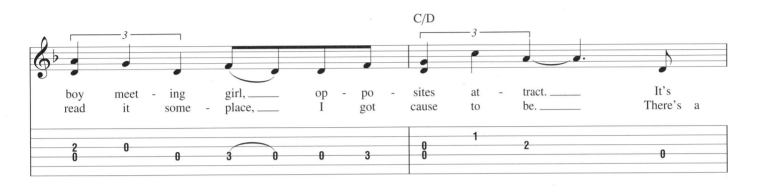

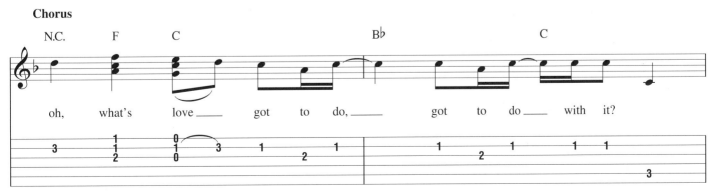

Chorus

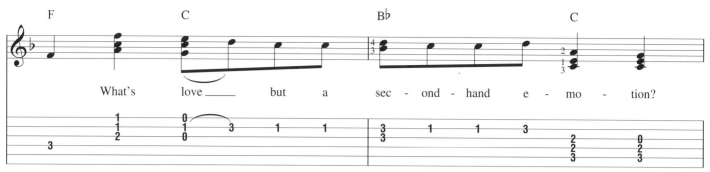

What's love _____ but a sec - ond - hand e - mo - tion?

What's love _____ got to do, _____ got to do _____ with it?

1.

Who needs a heart when a heart can be bro - ken? 2. It

2.

heart can be bro - ken?

Interlude

1., 2., 3.

4.

Bridge

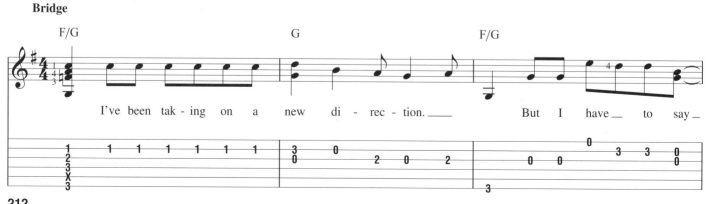

I've been tak - ing on a new di - rec - tion. _____ But I have _ to say _

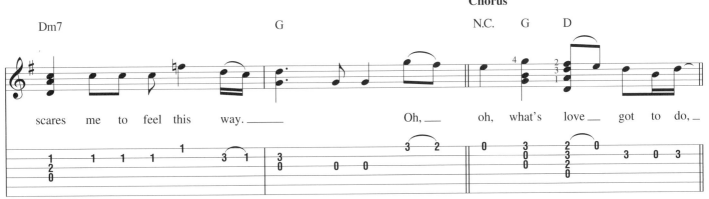

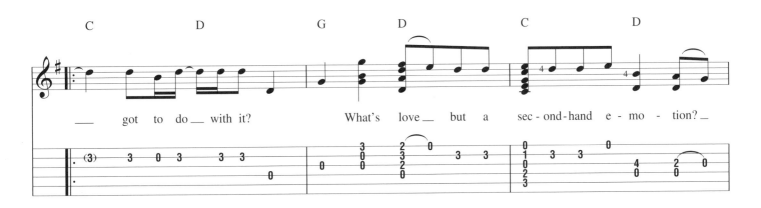

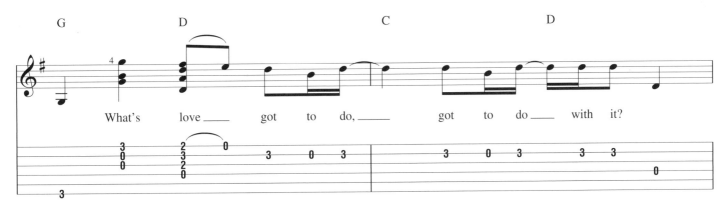

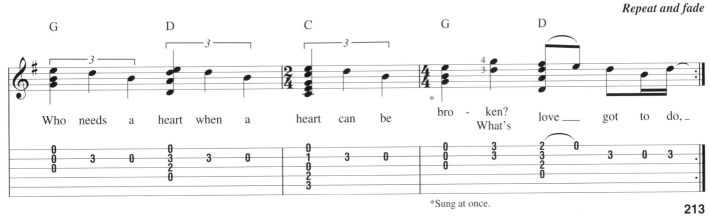

*Sung at once.

STRUM AND PICK PATTERNS

This chart contains the suggested strum and pick patterns that are referred to by number at the beginning of each song in this book. The symbols ⊓ and ∨ in the strum patterns refer to down and up strokes, respectively. The letters in the pick patterns indicate which right-hand fingers play which strings.

p = thumb
i = index finger
m = middle finger
a = ring finger

For example; Pick Pattern 2
is played: thumb - index - middle - ring

Strum Patterns

Pick Patterns

You can use the 3/4 Strum and Pick Patterns in songs written in compound meter (6/8, 9/8, 12/8, etc.). For example, you can accompany a song in 6/8 by playing the 3/4 pattern twice in each measure. The 4/4 Strum and Pick Patterns can be used for songs written in cut time (¢) by doubling the note time values in the patterns. Each pattern would therefore last two measures in cut time.

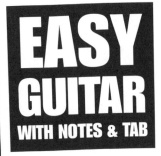

EASY GUITAR
WITH NOTES & TAB

This series features simplified arrangements with notes, tab, chord charts, and strum and pick patterns.

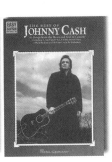

MIXED FOLIOS

00702287	Acoustic	$14.99
00702002	Acoustic Rock Hits for Easy Guitar	$12.95
00702166	All-Time Best Guitar Collection	$19.99
00699665	Beatles Best	$12.95
00702232	Best Acoustic Songs for Easy Guitar	$12.99
00702233	Best Hard Rock Songs	$14.99
00703055	The Big Book of Nursery Rhymes & Children's Songs	$14.99
00322179	The Big Easy Book of Classic Rock Guitar	$24.95
00698978	Big Christmas Collection	$16.95
00702394	Bluegrass Songs for Easy Guitar	$12.99
00703387	Celtic Classics	$14.99
00118314	Chart Hits of 2012-2013	$14.99
00702149	Children's Christian Songbook	$7.95
00702237	Christian Acoustic Favorites	$12.95
00702028	Christmas Classics	$7.95
00101779	Christmas Guitar	$14.99
00702185	Christmas Hits	$9.95
00702016	Classic Blues for Easy Guitar	$12.95
00702141	Classic Rock	$8.95
00702203	CMT's 100 Greatest Country Songs	$27.95
00702283	The Contemporary Christian Collection	$16.99
00702006	Contemporary Christian Favorites	$9.95
00702239	Country Classics for Easy Guitar	$19.99
00702282	Country Hits of 2009–2010	$14.99

00702240	Country Hits of 2007–2008	$12.95
00702225	Country Hits of '06–'07	$12.95
00702085	Disney Movie Hits	$12.95
00702257	Easy Acoustic Guitar Songs	$14.99
00702280	Easy Guitar Tab White Pages	$29.99
00702212	Essential Christmas	$9.95
00702041	Favorite Hymns for Easy Guitar	$9.95
00702281	4 Chord Rock	$9.99
00702286	Glee	$16.99
00699374	Gospel Favorites	$14.95
00702160	The Great American Country Songbook	$15.99
00702050	Great Classical Themes for Easy Guitar	$6.95
00702116	Greatest Hymns for Guitar	$8.95
00702130	The Groovy Years	$9.95
00702184	Guitar Instrumentals	$9.95
00702046	Hits of the '70s for Easy Guitar	$8.95
00702273	Irish Songs	$12.99
00702275	Jazz Favorites for Easy Guitar	$14.99
00702274	Jazz Standards for Easy Guitar	$14.99
00702162	Jumbo Easy Guitar Songbook	$19.95
00702258	Legends of Rock	$14.99
00702261	Modern Worship Hits	$14.99
00702189	MTV's 100 Greatest Pop Songs	$24.95
00702272	1950s Rock	$14.99
00702271	1960s Rock	$14.99
00702270	1970s Rock	$14.99

00702269	1980s Rock	$14.99
00702268	1990s Rock	$14.99
00109725	Once	$14.99
00702187	Selections from O Brother Where Art Thou?	$12.95
00702178	100 Songs for Kids	$12.95
00702515	Pirates of the Caribbean	$12.99
00702125	Praise and Worship for Guitar	$9.95
00702155	Rock Hits for Guitar	$9.95
00702285	Southern Rock Hits	$12.99
00702866	Theme Music	$12.99
00121535	30 Easy Celtic Guitar Solos	$14.99
00702124	Today's Christian Rock – 2nd Edition	$9.95
00702220	Today's Country Hits	$9.95
00702198	Today's Hits for Guitar	$9.95
00702217	Top Christian Hits	$12.95
00702235	Top Christian Hits of '07–'08	$14.95
00103626	Top Hits of 2012	$14.99
00702294	Top Worship Hits	$14.99
00702206	Very Best of Rock	$9.95
00702255	VH1's 100 Greatest Hard Rock Songs	$27.99
00702175	VH1's 100 Greatest Songs of Rock and Roll	$24.95
00702253	Wicked	$12.99

ARTIST COLLECTIONS

00702267	AC/DC for Easy Guitar	$15.99
00702598	Adele for Easy Guitar	$14.99
00702001	Best of Aerosmith	$16.95
00702040	Best of the Allman Brothers	$14.99
00702865	J.S. Bach for Easy Guitar	$12.99
00702169	Best of The Beach Boys	$12.99
00702292	The Beatles — 1	$19.99
00702201	The Essential Black Sabbath	$12.95
00702140	Best of Brooks & Dunn	$10.95
02501615	Zac Brown Band — The Foundation	$16.99
02501621	Zac Brown Band — You Get What You Give	$16.99
00702095	Best of Mariah Carey	$12.95
00702043	Best of Johnny Cash	$16.99
00702033	Best of Steven Curtis Chapman	$14.95
00702291	Very Best of Coldplay	$12.99
00702263	Best of Casting Crowns	$12.99
00702090	Eric Clapton's Best	$10.95
00702086	Eric Clapton — from the Album Unplugged	$10.95
00702202	The Essential Eric Clapton	$12.95
00702250	blink-182 — Greatest Hits	$12.99
00702053	Best of Patsy Cline	$10.95
00702229	The Very Best of Creedence Clearwater Revival	$14.99
00702145	Best of Jim Croce	$12.99
00702278	Crosby, Stills & Nash	$12.99
00702219	David Crowder*Band Collection	$12.95
00702122	The Doors for Easy Guitar	$12.99
00702276	Fleetwood Mac — Easy Guitar Collection	$12.99
00702190	Best of Pat Green	$19.95

00702136	Best of Merle Haggard	$12.99
00702243	Hannah Montana	$14.95
00702227	Jimi Hendrix — Smash Hits	$14.99
00702288	Best of Hillsong United	$12.99
00702236	Best of Antonio Carlos Jobim	$12.95
00702245	Elton John — Greatest Hits 1970–2002	$14.99
00702204	Robert Johnson	$9.95
00702277	Best of Jonas Brothers	$14.99
00702234	Selections from Toby Keith — 35 Biggest Hits	$12.95
00702003	Kiss	$9.95
00702193	Best of Jennifer Knapp	$12.95
00702216	Lynyrd Skynyrd	$15.99
00702182	The Essential Bob Marley	$12.95
00702346	Bruno Mars — Doo-Wops & Hooligans	$12.99
00702248	Paul McCartney — All the Best	$14.99
00702129	Songs of Sarah McLachlan	$12.95
02501316	Metallica — Death Magnetic	$15.95
00702209	Steve Miller Band — Young Hearts (Greatest Hits)	$12.95
00702096	Best of Nirvana	$14.95
00702211	The Offspring — Greatest Hits	$12.95
00702030	Best of Roy Orbison	$12.95
00702144	Best of Ozzy Osbourne	$14.99
00702279	Tom Petty	$12.99
00102911	Pink Floyd	$16.99
00702139	Elvis Country Favorites	$9.95
00702293	The Very Best of Prince	$12.99
00699415	Best of Queen for Guitar	$14.99
00109279	Best of R.E.M.	$14.99

00702208	Red Hot Chili Peppers — Greatest Hits	$12.95
00702093	Rolling Stones Collection	$17.95
00702092	Best of the Rolling Stones	$14.99
00702196	Best of Bob Seger	$12.95
00702252	Frank Sinatra — Nothing But the Best	$12.99
00702010	Best of Rod Stewart	$14.95
00702049	Best of George Strait	$12.95
00702259	Taylor Swift for Easy Guitar	$14.99
00702260	Taylor Swift – Fearless	$12.99
00115960	Taylor Swift — Red	$16.99
00702290	Taylor Swift — Speak Now	$14.99
00702223	Chris Tomlin — Arriving	$12.95
00702262	Chris Tomlin Collection	$14.99
00702226	Chris Tomlin — See the Morning	$12.95
00702427	U2 — 18 Singles	$14.99
00702108	Best of Stevie Ray Vaughan	$10.95
00702123	Best of Hank Williams	$12.99
00702111	Stevie Wonder — Guitar Collection	$9.95
00702228	Neil Young — Greatest Hits	$15.99
00119133	Neil Young – Harvest	$14.99
00702188	Essential ZZ Top	$10.95

Prices, contents and availability subject to change without notice.

HAL•LEONARD®
CORPORATION

7777 W. BLUEMOUND RD. P.O. BOX 13819 MILWAUKEE, WI 53213

Visit Hal Leonard online at
www.halleonard.com

0713

THE GRAMMY AWARDS®

SONGBOOKS FROM HAL LEONARD

These elite collections of the nominees and winners of
Grammy Awards since the honor's inception in 1958
provide a snapshot of the changing times in popular music.

PIANO/VOCAL/GUITAR

**GRAMMY AWARDS
RECORD OF THE YEAR
1958–2011**

Beat It • Beautiful Day •
Bridge over Troubled Water
• Don't Know Why • Don't
Worry, Be Happy • The Girl
from Ipanema (Garôta De
Ipanema) • Hotel California
• I Will Always Love You •
Just the Way You Are • Mack
the Knife • Moon River • My Heart Will Go on
(Love Theme from 'Titanic') • Rehab • Sailing •
Unforgettable • Up, Up and Away • The Wind Beneath
My Wings • and more.
00313603 P/V/G...................................... $19.99

**THE GRAMMY AWARDS
SONG OF THE YEAR
1958–1969**

Battle of New Orleans • Born
Free • Fever • The Good Life •
A Hard Day's Night • Harper
Valley P.T.A. • Hello, Dolly! •
Hey Jude • King of the Road
• Little Green Apples • Mrs.
Robinson • Ode to Billy Joe
• People • Somewhere, My
Love • Strangers in the Night • A Time for Us (Love
Theme) • Volare • Witchcraft • Yesterday • and more.
00313598 P/V/G...................................... $19.99

**THE GRAMMY AWARDS
SONG OF THE YEAR 1970–1979**

Alone Again (Naturally) • American Pie • At
Seventeen • Don't It Make My Brown Eyes Blue •
Honesty • (I Never Promised You A) Rose Garden •
I Write the Songs • Killing Me Softly with His Song •
Let It Be • Me and Bobby McGee • Send in the Clowns
• Song Sung Blue • Stayin' Alive • Three Times a Lady
• The Way We Were • You're So Vain • You've Got a
Friend • and more.
00313599 P/V/G...................................... $19.99

**THE GRAMMY AWARDS
SONG OF THE YEAR 1980–1989**

Against All Odds (Take a Look at Me Now) • Always
on My Mind • Beat It • Bette Davis Eyes • Don't Worry,
Be Happy • Ebony and Ivory • Endless Love • Every
Breath You Take • Eye of the Tiger • Fame • Fast Car
• Hello • I Just Called to Say I Love You • La Bamba
• Nine to Five • The Rose • Somewhere Out There •
Time After Time • We Are the World • and more.
00313600 P/V/G...................................... $19.99

**THE GRAMMY AWARDS
SONG OF THE YEAR 1990–1999**

Can You Feel the Love Tonight • (Everything I Do)
I Do It for You • From a Distance • Give Me One
Reason • I Swear • Kiss from a Rose • Losing My
Religion • My Heart Will Go on (Love Theme from
'Titanic') • Nothing Compares 2 U • Smooth • Streets
of Philadelphia • Tears in Heaven • Unforgettable
• Walking in Memphis • A Whole New World • You
Oughta Know • and more.
00313601 P/V/G...................................... $19.99

**THE GRAMMY AWARDS SONG
OF THE YEAR 2000–2009**

Beautiful • Beautiful Day • Breathe • Chasing
Pavements • Complicated • Dance with My Father •
Daughters • Don't Know Why • Fallin' • I Hope You
Dance • I'm Yours • Live like You Were Dying • Poker
Face • Rehab • Single Ladies (Put a Ring on It) • A
Thousand Miles • Umbrella • Use Somebody • Viva La
Vida • and more.
00313602 P/V/G...................................... $19.99

**THE GRAMMY AWARDS
BEST COUNTRY SONG 1964–2011**

Always on My Mind • Before He Cheats • Behind
Closed Doors • Bless the Broken Road • Butterfly
Kisses • Dang Me • Forever and Ever, Amen • The
Gambler • I Still Believe in You • I Swear • King of the
Road • Live like You Were Dying • Love Can Build a
Bridge • Need You Now • On the Road Again • White
Horse • You Decorated My Life • and more.
00313604 P/V/G...................................... $19.99

**THE GRAMMY AWARDS
BEST R&B SONG 1958–2011**

After the Love Has Gone • Ain't No Sunshine • Be
Without You • Billie Jean • End of the Road • Good
Golly Miss Molly • Hit the Road Jack • If You Don't
Know Me by Now • Papa's Got a Brand New Bag •
Respect • Shine • Single Ladies (Put a Ring on It) •
(Sittin' On) the Dock of the Bay • Superstition • U
Can't Touch This • We Belong Together • and more.
00313605 P/V/G...................................... $19.99

**THE GRAMMY AWARDS BEST POP
& ROCK GOSPEL ALBUMS (2000–2011)**

Call My Name • Come on Back to Me • Deeper Walk
• Forever • Gone • I Need You • I Smile • I Will Follow
• King • Leaving 99 • Lifesong • Looking Back at
You • Much of You • My Love Remains • Say So •
Somebody's Watching • Step by Step/Forever We Will
Sing • Tunnel • Unforgettable You • You Hold My World •
Your Love Is a Song • and more.
00313680 P/V/G...................................... $16.99

Prices, contents, and availabilibity subject to change without notice.

HAL•LEONARD® CORPORATION

7777 W. BLUEMOUND RD. P.O. BOX 13819 MILWAUKEE, WI 53213

www.halleonard.com

ELECTRONIC KEYBOARD

**THE GRAMMY AWARDS
RECORD OF THE YEAR
1958–2011 – VOL. 160**

All I Wanna Do • Bridge over
Troubled Water • Don't Know
Why • The Girl from Ipanema
(Garôta De Ipanema) • Hotel
California • I Will Always
Love You • Just the Way You
Are • Killing Me Softly with
His Song • Love Will Keep Us
Together • Rehab • Unforgettable • What's Love Got to
Do with It • The Wind Beneath My Wings • and more.
00100315 E-Z Play Today #160 .... $16.99

PRO VOCAL
WOMEN'S EDITIONS

**THE GRAMMY AWARDS
BEST FEMALE POP VOCAL
PERFORMANCE 1990–1999 — VOL. 57**

Book/CD Pack

All I Wanna Do • Building a Mystery • Constant
Craving • I Will Always Love You • I Will Remember
You • My Heart Will Go on (Love Theme from
'Titanic') • No More "I Love You's" • Something to Talk
About (Let's Give Them Something to Talk About) •
Unbreak My Heart • Vision of Love.
00740446 Melody/Lyrics/Chords................. $14.99

**THE GRAMMY AWARDS
BEST FEMALE POP VOCAL
PERFORMANCE 2000-2009 – VOL. 58**

Book/CD Pack

Ain't No Other Man • Beautiful • Chasing Pavements •
Don't Know Why • Halo • I Try • I'm like a Bird • Rehab
• Since U Been Gone • Sunrise.
00740447 Melody/Lyrics/Chords................. $14.99

MEN'S EDITIONS

**THE GRAMMY AWARDS
BEST MALE POP VOCAL
PERFORMANCE 1990-1999 – VOL. 59**

Book/CD Pack

Brand New Day • Can You Feel the Love Tonight •
Candle in the Wind 1997 • Change the World • If I
Ever Lose My Faith in You • Kiss from a Rose • My
Father's Eyes • Oh, Pretty Woman • Tears in Heaven •
When a Man Loves a Woman.
00740448 Melody/Lyrics/Chords................. $14.99

**THE GRAMMY AWARDS
BEST MALE POP VOCAL
PERFORMANCE 2000-2009 – VOL. 60**

Book/CD Pack

Cry Me a River • Daughters • Don't Let Me Be Lonely
Tonight • Make It Mine • Say • Waiting on the World
to Change • What Goes Around...Comes Around
Interlude • Your Body Is a Wonderland.
00740449 Melody/Lyrics/Chords................. $14.99